Presented To:

_____

Presented By:

_____

Date:

_____

# God's Little Devotional Book
## for Grandparents

An Imprint of Cook Communications Ministries
Colorado Springs, Colorado

07 06 05 04 03     10 9 8 7 6 5 4 3 2 1

## God's Little Devotional Book for Grandparents

ISBN 1-56292-602-0
Copyright © 2003 by Bordon Books
6532 East 71 Street, Suite 105
Tulsa, OK 74133

Published by Honor Books
An Imprint of Cook Communications Ministries
4050 Lee Vance View
Colorado Springs, Colorado 80918

Developed by Bordon Books

# Introduction

You are a grandparent now. All the experience and wisdom of your years is more valuable than ever. God designed your special gifts to be shared with others. As a result, your heartfelt gifts of love, joy, and wisdom naturally spill over into the lives of your children and grandchildren, no matter where they live, no matter how old they may be. At times, however, even grandparents may find themselves in need of encouragement and inspiration.

God's Little Devotional Book for Grandparents was written especially for people whom little ones call Grandma, Nana, Mimi, Grandpa, Papa, or Pop, and a myriad of other special names. As a grandparent, you will enjoy a tremendous amount of wit and wisdom as you browse through the inspirational quotes, captivating stories, and Scripture found in this delightful book.

From the funny stories grandchildren tell, to recollections of days gone by, heartwarming reflections will underline the importance of a grandparent's contribution to the lives of his or her grandchildren.

> Grandchildren are
> God's compensation
> for growing old.

Grandchildren should come with labeled warnings: May induce unrestrained laughter. May cause silly giggling. May create a smile when least expected. Laughing out loud is a common side effect of time spent with grandchildren.

Consider these examples:

Three generations sat down to dinner. The two grandsons tried to display their very best behavior when one of them let out a loud burp. "Peter," exclaimed the embarrassed mother, "you need to say excuse me."

"Why?" queried the wide-eyed boy, "Grandpa doesn't."

A small girl saw a Dalmatian dog for the first time. "Grandma," she inquired, "why is that dog wearing a cow?"

A concerned three-year-old boy asked his mother a very important question: "Mom, have I ever been married?"

A grandfather explained to his grandson why there were Vote Yes and Vote No signs around town. Pondering his grandpa's explanation, the small boy made a suggestion. "Let's vote maybe!"

A little girl met her infant cousin for the first time. "When he gets older, will he speak English?" she asked.

A visiting grandmother said bedtime prayers with her pint-sized grandson. He wiggled and squirmed and then asked, "Grandma can you please hurry up? You're spitting on me!"

Laughing with the grandchildren is one of a grandparent's greatest rewards. Be sure you laugh with yours.

Children's children are a crown to the aged.
PROVERBS 17:6

Most people will readily agree that a butterfly in flight is a truly beautiful sight. However, the gradual transformation from egg to caterpillar, to cocoon to butterfly, can easily be overlooked. In fact, this process can seem so tedious and unattractive that most people prefer to ignore it and simply admire the final creation. But to any true nature-lover, the process is just as awe-inspiring and breathtaking as the end product—the glorious butterfly.

> A grandparent's eyes see miracles where others see messes.

The same is true for grandparents. To others, the various stages of a grandchild's development may seem boring and at times unattractive. The tantrums, whining, crying, and incessant questioning can seem aggravating and inconvenient.

With God's help, grandparents can look at the growth of a child through His eyes. They can enjoy the growing-up process and feel privileged to be a vital part of the lives of their grandchildren.

As grandparents, we should look for opportunities to teach the grandkids valuable lessons about God's nature. We should also impress upon them the importance of imitating Christ in all they do. Grandparents should choose to be active participants in the lives of the grandchildren. They should observe them as they grow older and rejoice when they come to know the Lord in a personal way.

At that time, grandparents will be able to sit back in awe, watch the lives of their grandchildren unfold, and show pride in the godly creations they have become. God will enable them to soar higher than the grandparents ever imagined. Their lives, like the butterflies, will add beauty to the world.

Let us not become weary in doing good,
for at the proper time we will reap
a harvest if we do not give up.
GALATIANS 6:9

> No one is quicker on the draw
> than a grandparent pulling
> pictures from a wallet.

His hand grasped for the billfold as he walked across the room. Carl's wallet fanned open like a propeller on an airplane before his friends could even ask to see a picture of his new granddaughter.

Amanda's arrival was the answer to many prayers sent up to Heaven by Carl's son and daughter-in-law. They tried for years to become pregnant, but each month brought discouragement and heart-wrenching disappointment.

After many years of soul-searching, the couple considered adoption. Unfortunately, adoption had its own painful experience as years of waiting turned into frustration and grief. A match with a birth mother fell through when the baby's biological father desired custody of the unborn child. Another birth mother stole money from Carl's son and daughter-in-law, so they felt they needed to end the adoption process.

When hope began to diminish, a birth mother chose the couple to become the parents of her child. All of the details fell into place. Amanda arrived on Carl's birthday. She immediately became the most thrilling addition to the family. Carl beamed with pride each time he relayed this story to friends and acquaintances. They looked down at the picture of the two-week-old baby girl who had been the answer to so many prayers.

"She is now ten weeks old," Carl mused, staring at the newborn picture. "And I'm her favorite Papa."

Grandchildren grant bragging rights, and no one is ever offended.

> Show me your face . . .
> your face is lovely.
> SONG OF SONGS 2:14

Twelve-year-old Sarah sat in rapt attention, listening to her great-grandpa's stories. He told her about growing up in a family so poor that he received only oranges for Christmas presents. He explained how when his parents couldn't afford to buy him a bicycle, he tried to make one out of spare parts he had found in a junkyard. When he told her about how he rode his horse, King, to school, she was bewildered.

"Your family didn't even have a car?" she asked. "When were you born, Popaw?"

He chuckled, crossed his arms around his round belly, and said with pride, "1910."

A grandparent is a living history lesson.

"Wow!" Sarah exclaimed. Her mouth dropped open in amazement.

"Pretty old, huh?" he grinned. He named some of the technological inventions that had come into existence during his lifetime. Electric lights, cars, planes, radios, telephones, televisions, computers, and cell phones were a few things that he listed.

"Yeah, I've sure seen a lot of changes," he explained. "Some have been good, and some have been bad. But through it all, I've learned that the one constant in this world is God. Whenever I'm worried or frightened, I stop to talk to Him. God is unchanging and completely dependable. You will probably face a lot of changes in your life, too, honey. But no matter what happens, remember to hold on to the Lord, for you can always count on Him to stay the same."

This grandfather understood that the history that would affect Sarah the most was the history of his personal walk with God. What about you? Have you shared this most important part of your history with your grandchildren?

I will instruct you and teach
you in the way you should go.
PSALM 32:8

13

## What is a grandmother?

Someone who puts a sweater
on you when she is cold,
feeds you when she is hungry,
and puts you to bed when she is tired.

The Mason family entertained three house-guests for four days. Sarah was a beautiful and charming young lady, who expected each member of the Mason household to meet her every need.

The other two houseguests made their beds and kept their rooms somewhat orderly. Not so with Sarah, however. She never made her bed. Her belongs were strewn all over the house.

The entire family went to a lovely restaurant for dinner during the stay. Sarah seemed unimpressed by the excellent food and service. She hardly touched her food and was noisier than anyone at the surrounding tables. At the close of her visit, Sarah left without as much as a thank you.

The very next weekend, nine-month-old Sarah was welcomed back into the Mason home again, regardless of her previous behavior. Her grandparents looked forward to each of her visits. Sarah didn't verbally express her gratitude like her older siblings. Her thank you came in the form of a beautiful smile to open the day and a big hug to begin the nighttime hours. Her very presence was gratitude enough.

What a wonderful way for a small child to say thank you! What an honor to be the grandparent and the recipient of that special showing of gratitude!

"It is more blessed to give than to receive."
ACTS 20:35

Carrie was exasperated with her two sons, Cody and Logan. She called her mom for moral support. "These two boys act just like Dennis the Menace," she fumed. She went on to explain the day's happenings. "The boys wanted to slide across the kitchen floor. It wasn't slippery enough to suit them, so they poured red drink crystals on the linoleum. They ran and slid onto the carpeting wearing their red stained socks, making a terrible mess. Later in the day, they discovered a can of bug spray," Carrie continued. "They went into the laundry room, climbed up on the dryer, and coated the walls with the nauseous liquid.

Certain personality traits are thought to skip a generation. Maybe that's why grandchildren and grandparents get along so well.

"Yesterday they filled the sink with water. When it began to overflow, they grabbed the trash can to catch the water. When it was full, they just splashed about while it poured out onto the floor."

It was easy for the grandmother to see the humor in the boys' antics, but she refrained from laughter. Instead her quiet and calm voice came shining through. Her wisdom spoke to Carrie's heart. "Honey, my pastor once said that when your patience is being tried, God is trying to show you something in your character. Many times I have had to remember those words myself."

Carrie thought about what her mother had said as she cleaned up the latest mess her sons had made. She considered the times that she had been less than perfect. She thought about the heartbreaking divorce, her credit-card problems, and the years she spent away from Lord.

"Heavenly Father," she whispered, "please don't ever give up on me or get tired of helping me clean up my life."

This grandparent's perspective shaped by time made her able to give wise counsel. Your own perspective has been years in the making. Share it with your children and grandchildren.

You have given me the heritage
of those who fear your name.
PSALM 61:5

## Grandparenting isn't

## for sissies.

Gabe and Beth looked forward to a slower pace. Their oldest son had moved out of state and had a good job. Their daughter, Mandy, recently started college and moved into a small apartment with her baby. Gabe and Beth had one teenage son living at home. The plans they had made for their retirement were bright. Unfortunately, peace and quiet was not ahead for them or for their family.

Mandy, who had become a mother at seventeen, wasn't handling the situations of life very well. She had cut several of her college classes. She wasn't showing up at work either. The situation continued to worsen as time went on. Gabe and Beth found it necessary to take their eighteen-month-old grandson into their home, changing their own future plans drastically.

"We have a sixteen-year-old at home, and now we are starting all over with a baby!" Beth lamented during her prayer time. "God, this is not what we wanted during this particular season of our lives."

Although their retirement years were not as they had expected, the couple adjusted to life with a lively toddler. There were smiles and giggles where silence would have been. Toys and books sat where order would have ruled. Love and affection lived where the empty hollow of time would have hung.

This setup wasn't what the couple had planned for their retirement. But God's plans for them were bigger and better. He sent abundant blessings their way in the form of a precious grandchild to enjoy every day of their retirement.

Act with courage, and may the
LORD be with those who do well.
2 CHRONICLES 19:11

Corrie ten Boom, the well-known author of In My Father's House, carried out a ministry that touched many nations. Until the ripe age of fifty, she led the quiet life of an unmarried woman.

Corrie resided with her father and sister above their watch shop in Haarlem, Holland. When not repairing watches, Corrie hosted Bible studies, led women's groups, and worked with needy children. Corrie and her family often "adopted" unwanted foster children and displaced refugees. They eventually hosted Jews. She shared her faith openly and often, as did her godly father, Casper ten Boom. Her simple life was filled with love, hope, and peace until the onset of World War II.

> Grandparents should remember this truth: unless you're made of cheese, age doesn't matter.

At that time, she and her family became prisoners of war. The years following were filled with much hurt and frustration. And often Corrie had to fight her own impulses to be angry and hate.

At the war's end, Corrie was released from the concentration camp where her sister Betsie and her father had perished. She then began a traveling ministry that encompassed over sixty countries. She wrote books, contributed to a monthly magazine, appeared on television, and interviewed on the radio. Her book, The Hiding Place, was made into a movie. She began her active ministry at an age when most people would say it was time to slow down.

The reason that Corrie continued to tell the story of Jesus, even into her eightieth year, was simple. For God so loved the world . . . (John 3:16). She had learned this love the hard way. And people of all ages needed to be told.

Never lose faith in the value God has invested in you. Even your mistakes are gold to Him. Don't neglect to invest that value in the lives of others—especially your grandchildren.

The eyes of the Lord keep watch over knowledge.

PROVERBS 22:12

> Nothing makes a boy
> smarter than being
> a grandson.

Brad and his brother loved their grandparents dearly. The boys spent as much time as possible with them after the grandparents retired. Grandma and Pop adored them, as well. The relationship between the four of them was indescribably rich. Pop spent hours teaching the boys important truths about life and love.

When Brad moved away from home to attend college, he initially lived in his grandparent's basement. Their relationship grew even closer during the months that they lived in the same house together.

Shortly after he retired, Brad's grandfather became ill. The family was forced to place Pop in a nursing home, so he could receive proper care.

Then Brad met the love of his life. A few months later, he bought her an engagement ring. When Brad picked it up, he drove straight from the jewelry store to the nursing home to show it to Pop first. Pop smiled as he understood what the ring meant. Even though he couldn't verbalize his feelings, his smile said everything that needed to be spoken.

Unfortunately, Pop didn't live long enough to attend Brad's wedding. Brad relished the fact, however, that his loving grandfather had been the first to know that he was engaged and that he also had been the first to see the ring that would be placed on his bride's finger. Because his grandfather had invested time and love into Brad's life, Brad wanted to share this most important event with him.

Spend time with your grandchildren and teach them what love looks like.

Cast your bread on the surface of the waters,
for you will find it after many days.
ECCLESIASTES 11:1 NASB

Do you have a hard time keeping up with all of your grandchildren? How many kids can you call your grandchildren now? Is it six, or could it be seven? When is the next one due? Does Christy spell her name Kristy, Christie, Khristy, or Cristee? Is Michael the oldest, or is it Stephen? Does Billy Bob play with only environmentally sound, non-chemical toys, or is that Summer Sky?

When asked if she had a hard time organizing all of her grandchildren, a grandma joked, "Actually, I think they have a hard time keeping up with me. For my birthday they gave me a shower radio. Now do you think I want to be dancing on a wet floor next to a glass door? The next year they presented me with a CD player. I just got over having to throw

> If you can't recall a grandchild's name, "Dear" or "Sweetie" will do just fine.

away all of my eight tracks, and now no more tapes to wind and rewind! I have received gift certificates for country line dancing, a leg waxing, and a makeover. Are they trying to tell me I need to shape up, clean up, and get made-up?"

Even if you can't keep them all straight, while you're kissing rosy cheeks, reading stories, playing cards, and cheering at soccer games, the grandchildren don't care. They see God's love shining through you. And they are more than proud to call you their grandparent.

Do everything in love.

1 CORINTHIANS 16:14

GLDB

> A grandparent is a
> baby-sitter who watches
> the kids, not the television.

"At my grandmother's kitchen table, I learned a lot about life and love," a young woman shared at a church conference. "Grandmother always had a way of making me feel special and important. Cooking and baking was one way she conveyed that to me. Many times I helped her measure out and combine the ingredients of a particular dish.

"As I stood on the wooden stool and stirred the contents in the bowl, I told her about my seven-year-old world of toys and friends. She told me funny stories about my mom when she was a little girl. While we were cleaning up, she let me know the importance of not just doing a job, but doing it well. And as we shared some of the cookies we baked with a few shut-ins in the neighborhood, I learned about caring for others.

"Now that I have children of my own, I better understand a few things. I am sure it took a lot longer to bake the cookies while I was there helping her. Certainly, there was a much bigger mess to clean up. The cookies were probably not as perfect as they could have been if she had just gone ahead and done it on her own. But I also know that it wasn't baking cookies that Grandmother was concerned about. It was all about bonding with me."

God's hands can often look a lot like Grandma's.

> Older women likewise are to be
> reverent in their behavior . . .
> teaching what is good.
> TITUS 2:3 NASB

A mother was teaching her child to recite the Lord's Prayer. After they had gone over the words a few times, the small boy rushed over to his daddy. "Daddy listen to me pray," he said excitedly. " . . . as we forgive those who trespass against us, and lead us not into temptation, but deliver us from e-mail."

A three-year-old little girl returned from her church preschool class and was anxious to recite the Lord's Prayer for her mom and dad. "Our father who does art in Heaven, Howard is his name."

> Grandparents are God's appointed prayer warriors for their grandchildren!

A six-year-old boy tried to grasp how to pray on his own. His mom told him repeatedly, "Honey, just say the same words Mommy does."

"I can say the blessing," the boy announced while sitting around the table with their dinner guests.

His proud mother beamed, "Sure honey, that would be fine."

"Dear God," he recited. "Thank You for this food before us. Lord, why did these people have to come to dinner tonight? Amen."

God listens to the prayers of both little people and big people. Thankfully, when we pray God listens to our hearts, not necessarily our words. Pray for your grandchildren—God will see the love and concern in your heart for them.

Don't worry about anything;
instead, pray about everything.
PHILIPPIANS 4:6 TLB

Grandparents are folks who come to your house, spoil your children, and then go home.

Brenda was feeling a bit frustrated. She shared her concerns with her wise Aunt Bessie. "John's parents are coming again this Easter. They always come armed with lollipops, homemade gingerbread cookies, licorice sticks, and peppermint drops. Their car will be loaded down with new storybooks, Barbie dolls, racing cars, basketballs, and a 1,342-piece army solider set!

"The last time they were visiting, they babysat while John and I went out," Brenda continued. Aunt Bessie listened carefully. "Do you know what happened while we were away? The children didn't go to bed on time. They forgot to brush their teeth. They didn't put on their pajamas. And to top it off, I found them sleeping on the family-room floor!

"I asked Brett why he was not in his bed. 'I fell asleep while Grandpa was wrestling with me,' he explained."

The young mother continued to complain. "And I have noticed that when they offer to take the family out to eat, they insist on letting the kids have unlimited soda and messy desserts like hot-fudge sundaes with whipped cream."

Aunt Bessie patted the young mother's hand, "I understand," she said wisely, "but years from now, your children will have the most wonderful memories of their grandparents. They will have priceless stories to tell their own children."

The memories that grandparents make never fade away. They are a blessing from God that lasts for many generations.

He blesses the home of the righteous.
PROVERBS 3:33

Michael sat in the nursing-home room spoon-feeding his grandfather ice cream. A nurse's aide noticed that he came to visit on a regular basis. One day she asked him about his obvious dedication to his grandfather.

"My grandfather never could find his glasses," Michael explained. "He always remembered the time I rolled his new Cadillac down the driveway into the neighbor's trashcans, however. He was always ready and willing to share the story with others. Grandpa remembered every one of my birthdays too. Even though five dollars doesn't go very far anymore, I could count on getting the gift he had to offer. My grandmother was a lot like him. At Christmas she remembered to bring us

> A grandparent remembers hundreds of "true" stories—whether they happened or not.

gifts. But she often forgot that very few of us like to wear homemade sweaters.

"When I was a kid, my grandparents came to my baseball and soccer games," Michael continued. "I can see them now, sitting in their lawn chairs and big goofy hats waving at me. They made it to every church production, school play, and high school debate championship. They attended my college graduation and my wedding. They have met all three of my sons. They gave me their time and their unconditional love. Now it is my turn to give something back in return."

The principles of seedtime and harvest, of sowing and reaping, of giving and receiving, always stand true and will last for generations to come. Sow the seed of your love into your grandchildren's lives.

You will always reap what you sow!

GALATIANS 6:7 NLT

> Grandchildren and grandparents
> get along so well because they
> often have a common simplicity.

A four-year-old boy was asked to act as the ring bearer in a relative's wedding. When the big day finally arrived, he carefully tugged the miniature tuxedo into place. The music began, and the boy started his diminutive march down the aisle. At first he just stared wide-eyed at the job before him. A few minutes later, he did something quite peculiar. After each step, he turned around, threw his hands up in the air, and yelled, "Grrr."

The congregation that had assembled for the wedding started to giggle and soon was reduced to tears laughing at the strange antics of this handsome little boy. The small figure continued his path down the aisle with a step and a "Grrr," a step and a "Grrr." When the boy finally reached the pulpit he was quite upset.

His grandfather leaned down and whispered, "Buddy, what are you doing? What is wrong?"

The little boy tearfully replied. "Why is everybody laughing at me? I was just trying to be the ring bear."

Just as we treasure a child's simplicity, God loves it when we are honest and straightforward with Him. Have you felt misunderstood lately? Has someone laughed at you? Are you confused or apprehensive about the tasks before you? At any age, we can come before Him with a childlike heart to receive comfort and wisdom.

"Anyone who will not receive the kingdom of God like a little child will never enter it."

MARK 10:15

Nine-month-old Hannah was spending the night with her grandparents. She woke up during the night and cried for her midnight bottle. Nana got up and warmed a bottle. Hannah drank a portion of her formula and then quickly fell back asleep. Nana placed the half-filled bottle on the bedside table.

The next morning when Hannah awoke, she spied the bottle containing the remainder of the formula. She reached for it. Nana knew that the milk would be spoiled by that time. She asked Hannah's grandfather, Pa, to go warm another bottle. The impatient Hannah begged for the bottle the entire time that Pa was gone. She didn't understand that Pa was preparing a fresh bottle that would be good for her. Nor did she

**Happy homes are built with blocks of patience.**

understand that the bottle that she was crying for could make her sick. Hannah wanted her bottle, and she wanted it right that second. She didn't hesitate to make her wishes known, as she screamed at the top of her lungs.

Sometimes as impatient adults, we treat God much the same way. We let Him know what we want without considering that our wants might not be good for us. The entire time that we are showing our impatience toward God, He may be preparing something even better for us. We pitch our adult fits, thinking we know best. Only God sees the big picture, and He is always faithful to give us exactly what we need.

"Do not worry about your life,
what you will eat or drink."
Matthew 6:25

> Don't just give your
> grandchildren good advice;
> give them good memories.

"During WWII, Grace spent every weekday after school sitting with her wonderful grandma. Grandma suffered from a severe case of diabetes. The disease had taken a toll on her body. It claimed her sight. One of her legs was in bad shape. She could only sit in her chair and look out the window.

Grandma's spirit was high during the hours that Grace spent with her. She looked forward to Grace's arrival each day. Grandma literally beamed as she asked Grace about her day at school. She was genuinely interested in Grace's life. Grandma eagerly listened to whatever happenings that Grace chose to share with her. Grandma had mastered the art of listening.

Grace was fourteen years old when her grandmother died. Sixty years later, Grace continues to remember her vividly. Grace felt special when she was in the presence of her grandmother. She attributes the self-esteem that she held during her entire lifetime to her grandmother's great love and undivided attention.

Grandparents can be some of the greatest listeners of all time. When your grandchildren want to share a special event in their lives with someone who cares, do they seek you out? Be a grandparent with a heart of gold, ears that are ready to listen, and hugs that say you care.

The memory of the righteous
will be a blessing.
PROVERBS 10:7

If you could read the minds of your grandchildren, these are some of the things you might expect to hear:

*I wonder why Grandma and Grandpa always have money for an ice cream cone when my mom is always broke?*

*Why does Grandma save the wrapping paper and ribbon from every present that she opens?*

*Grandpa doesn't have a job. I wonder if Grandma knows.*

*Every time Mom and Dad go out on a date, Grandma and Grandpa show up for a visit!*

*Why do my grandparents keep my baby pictures in their living room? Haven't they noticed that I'm much bigger now?*

*My grandpa can fix* anything. *I wonder how he got so smart?*

> The heart of a grandchild records faithfully the scenes from a grandparent's life.

*And if Grandpa's so smart, how come when I ask him where babies come from, he says he can't remember? I wonder if he remembers where he got Mom.*

*Grandma and Grandpa come to all of my soccer games. They even went to my sister's piano recital. They must really love us!*

*Grandma told me that she prays for me every day. I hope God doesn't get tired of hearing about me.*

*How does Grandma always know when I need a hug and a kiss?*

*Why does Grandma let me kiss her when I have chocolate on my face?*

When you are a big part of your grand-children's lives, you are a big part of their thoughts as well.

*The secret things belong to the LORD our God, but the things revealed belong to us and to our children forever, that we may follow all the words of this law.*

DEUTERONOMY 29:29

> You may have more grandchildren
> than you can name, but never
> more than you can love!

"I'm everybody's grandmother," said Barbara Bush. On January 20, 1989, this mother of five and grandmother to eleven became the first lady of the United States. Her position as first lady allowed her to work on community projects, host many social affairs, and meet famous and influential people. Her passion was to share her lifelong interest in working with those who could not read.

Barbara Bush felt that many of society's ills were the direct result of the inability to understand the words on a printed page. Her interest began in her own family when she discovered that her son had a reading problem. She worked with Neil for many years to help him become the fantastic reader that he is today.

The Barbara Bush Foundation for Family Literacy supplies money for special reading programs. Its primary function is to "help every family in the nation understand that home is the child's first school, and the parent is the child's first teacher, and reading is the child's first subject."

Now that she and her husband are retired, they have more time to spend with their grandchildren. They often host family gatherings with three generations around them. To them Barbara has always been the "first lady" of the Bush family.

Love comes in many forms. Hugs and kisses tell others that we love them. Holding a grandchild on one's lap and reading a story is another special way that a grandmother can show the depth of her love.

*"A new command I give you:*
*Love one another. As I have loved you,*
*so you must love one another."*
JOHN 13:34

A grandmother agreed to keep her three-year-old grandson, Josh, for a few days. It had been a number of years since a child had stayed overnight in her house. She assured her daughter and son-in-law that she could handle a little boy. *How much trouble could he be,* she wondered? *He is so cute and innocent.*

Grandma was in the laundry room folding clothes when Josh decided he was hungry. She had baked cookies with him earlier that morning. Without thinking, she had left the brown sugar on the edge of the counter in the kitchen. She walked across the wooden floor to check on him. When she felt the grit under her feet, she realized that she had a mess to clean up.

> The quickest way to get a grandchild's attention is to sit down and look comfortable.

The next day Josh found the large plastic bottle of baby powder that his grandmother had left out in the guest room. The once blue carpet became a frosty white. Josh resembled Frosty the Snowman. The next day he did it again!

Saturday morning, Grandma and Grandpa slept in a little too late and awoke to find a chair pushed up to the counter and an entire box of cereal poured out and smashed onto the kitchen floor. Though Grandma discovered her grandson to be a much busier toddler than she recalled his mother as having been when she was a child, she lifted him up for a big hug.

The Bible tells us, "Love covers a multitude of sins" (1 Peter 4:8 NRSV). With a grandmother and a grandson, love also covers a multitude of messes.

*Accept one another, then,*
*just as Christ accepted you,*
*in order to bring praise to God.*
ROMANS 15:7

> Loving a grandchild is circular:
> the more love you give,
> the more you get—and the
> more you want to give again.

A farmer posted a sign Puppies for Sale. Early the next morning, he spotted a young boy walking slowly up the dusty trail to his farm.

"Hello, son," the farmer announced. "What can I do for you?"

"I heard you have some puppies for sale, and I've got forty-five cents to spend."

The farmer scratched his head. These puppies were purebred and could be sold for a lot more than forty-five cents. The freckle-faced boy looked up and grinned. The farmer thought of his own grandson's pleasure with the many litters of puppies they'd had on the farm over the years. He found himself calling the puppies over.

"Skipper, Skipper." Soon the pile of fur, teeth, and lolling tongues came rolling out in a pile. The young boy squealed with delight and tried petting them all simultaneously. Just behind the heap of dogs came the last pup, a runt, who didn't scamper, but slowly trudged along.

The boy gasped, "That's the one!"

"No, son, something's wrong with this puppy's legs. He wouldn't be a good choice." The boy pulled up his own pant-legs and exposed the steel braces that glistened in the sun.

"But sir, there is something wrong with my legs too, so we're a perfect match."

The farmer fingered the forty-five cents in his hand as he watched the two new friends as they walked down the driveway. The two of them were a match made in Heaven.

God is a matchmaker. He unites men and women. He joins orphans with parents. He brings families together. And He even creates the perfect matches with kids and grandparents. Think about the ways He has matched you with your grandchildren and thank Him.

*Keep yourselves in God's love as you wait for the mercy of our Lord Jesus Christ to bring you to eternal life.*
JUDE 1:21

There is a story told of Tito, the iron-fisted communist ruler of Yugoslavia. When he was a young boy in his small country village, he served as an alter boy for a new, young priest. During the service, the nervous Tito accidentally dropped the red flask of wine. The accident reverberated with a loud crash, and a bright crimson stain appeared on the cold marble floor. The red-faced priest became furious at the embarrassment caused in front of his congregation. He shouted abruptly at Tito. "Leave and never come back!"

> Grandchildren need love—especially when they don't deserve it.

Archbishop Fulton Sheen had a similar experience, but one exemplifying more of God's grace. As a youngster, he also served as an alter boy. While assisting a bishop during a worship service, he fumbled the wine and created a dripping mess. He nervously looked up at the important bishop expecting his deserved criticism. Instead the kindly collared man leaned down and whispered something in his ear. "It's OK, someday you, too, will be a priest." And later on, his words were fulfilled.

Grandchildren need our constant encouragement and love. You can never be sure who may have spoken harshly or uttered an unkind word to your grandchild. In your care, however, you can gently build them back up with your compassionate words and deeds.

*Above all these put on love, which binds everything together in perfect harmony.*
COLOSSIANS 3:14 RSV

GLDB

> # Love is a great present,
>
> # and it's always returnable.

Evan's older sister needed a blood transfusion. He had recently recovered from the same rare disease that his pale, small sister now struggled to defeat. The only treatment for this rare disease was a blood transfusion from a person who had already overcome the affliction. Since they both had the same rare blood type, her brother seemed to be the perfect donor.

When the parents asked Evan if he would like to give his blood to his sickly sister, he hesitated, stared off into space for just a moment, and then said, "Sure."

The next day Evan and his sister went to a large medical center to perform the life-saving blood transfusion. On the way, Evan and his sister giggled and fidgeted together. As soon as the nurse began to prepare for the procedure, however, they both settled down.

For someone so young and full of energy, the young boy seemed to be very quiet during the whole process. The nurse was concerned about his quietness and allowed his parents and grandfather into the room.

"Are you OK, Evan?" his grandfather inquired.

Evan slowly nodded. Then he whispered, "When do I die, Grandpa?"

The grandfather smiled and looked deep into his grandson's eyes. "Son, you're not going to die. They won't take all of your blood. Your sister only needs a little bit of your blood to help her get better. You will be just fine."

Evan's mother reassured him with a nod of her head and a hug.

Evan's grandfather slowly slipped out of the room with his own son. Tears clouded his eyes as he spoke to him, "Evan was willing to die so that his sister could live."

Jesus loved us enough to die for us. While few on this earth are called to that level of commitment, we are called daily to give to others.

*May the Lord make your love increase*
*and overflow for each other.*

1 THESSALONIANS 3:12

The two-year-old child had no arms. His legs were only developed to the thighs. To make matters worse, he was also completely blind. A social worker was sent to the child's home to perform an evaluation. When she entered the home, she met both the child and his grandmother, the caretaker of the baby. She fully expected to see a lifeless baby in a crib. Instead she found a squealing, gurgling, active little boy. His grandmother swooped him into her arms and brushed the dark hair off his face. She smiled brightly.

> A grandparent is a builder of dreams and a sculptor of souls.

"This is my Christopher," the grandmother announced enthusiastically.

"She was as proud as any grandmother I have ever met," the social worker admitted.

As she began her evaluation, the social worker was amazed at how interested the child was in her, even though she was a stranger. She shook bells, put a hat on his head, and gave him toys to hold between his stunted arms. He greeted each task with enthusiasm. She played music and watched as he rocked back and forth. She brushed a feather on his neck and face, and he squealed with delight. The whole time she was there, his grandmother beamed with gladness over his accomplishments.

When a grandmother believes in and shows pride in her grandchildren, marvelous miracles are sure to occur.

*We speak of God's secret wisdom, a wisdom that has been hidden and that God destined for our glory before time began.*
1 CORINTHIANS 2:7

A popular car tag specifically
for grandparents, simply states,
"Let me tell you about my grandchildren."

Religion columnist and author Nancy B. Gibbs writes often about her granddaughter, Hannah. Even at only eighteen months of age, Hannah's actions demonstrate many spiritual truths. Nancy finds it easy to capture her precious actions on paper, much like many people capture moments in time on video cameras.

Many times after an article about Hannah is featured as her weekly column, the people in her community will stop Nancy to ask how Hannah is doing or to let her know that the article touched them in a particular way. Hannah's precious tactics have brightened many people's lives through the written word.

Grandchildren have a way of teaching spiritual truths in everyday living. A grandparent should be the most knowledgeable and inspired person around. The innocence of a child is sure to shine through all difficulties, especially to a grandparent who thinks the child can do no wrong.

It is obvious by the stories she shares that Nancy is truly in love with the little girl in her life. After every visit with her precious granddaughter, Nancy has a new article to write and a fresh story to tell.

A story told by a grandparent never grows old, never goes out of style, and is certain to bring joy to the hearts of readers of all ages. There's something special about the opportunity to share happy thoughts about a grandchild and also in the hearing of the stories that bring so much pleasure to a grandparent's life.

*I am sending him to you for this
very purpose, that you may know how
we are, and that he may encourage you.*
EPHESIANS 6:22

Karen loved to talk about her kindly grandfather who was saved late in life. "Grandpa Bradbury became a Christian at the age of sixty-five," she shared. "But he lived the years he had left with a tremendous fire to share the Gospel with others.

"After Grandpa Bradbury received the Lord, he visited the Cook County Hospital wards on a regular basis. For twenty years, he presented three-minute gospel messages to the sick people resting on the rows of white hospital beds." Karen continued, "Grandpa had many heart problems. While he received treatment, he witnessed to every nurse and doctor that he met. He eventually led his cardiac physician, Dr. Donahue, to Christ. After Grandpa's death, Dr. Donahue told our

> A grandparent is a sustaining influence in a child's life and a forever love in a child's heart.

family that with Grandpa's heart damage, he should have died years earlier. Dr. Donahue believed, however, that God kept Grandpa alive, so he could continue to preach the Gospel to as many people as possible."

Karen wrote a song about her grandfather:

You were my grandpa and a very close friend,
    living for Jesus until the end.
    Even though you were old and gray,
    you would always faithfully say:
    "Jesus is my strength and He is my joy,
    this mouth of mine will I always employ
    in speaking the Gospel loud and clear,
    for it is God's will for everyone to hear!"

*Encourage one another daily,*
*as long as it is called Today.*
HEBREWS 3:13

> Grandma and Grandpa's house:
> where the great are small,
> and the small are great.

A grandma enjoyed telling this humorous story:

"We were paying a visit with my daughter, her husband, and their ten children. My husband and I lingered over coffee at the kitchen table as our grandchildren came in and out of the kitchen to eat breakfast. Westin, the youngest of the ten, bounded into the kitchen, proudly waving a crisp one-dollar bill.

"'Look Grandma!' he shouted. 'Look what the tooth fairy brought me.'

"*My—how times have changed,* I thought. *My kids only received a dime in exchange for their teeth.*

"About that time, I noticed an exchange between my daughter and her husband. They were staring at each other mouthing these words:

"'Did you?'

"'No!'

"'Did you?'

"'Me neither!'

"'Well, maybe there is something to this tooth fairy after all!' my daughter whispered to her husband.

"When young Westin left the room, Kevin, who was fourteen years old and sixth or seventh in line, explained how the dollar got under Westin's pillow.

"'It was me, Mom. I just thought you would probably be too busy to remember. So I took care of it for you.'

The grandmother's eyes shone as she hugged Kevin for his thoughtfulness. She made up her mind to pay attention to small things in her grandchildren's lives as Kevin had for his brother.

Servants usually do not do impressive or grand things. Rather it is in the little things that they do their best service.

*"Whoever wishes to become great among you shall be your servant."*
MATTHEW 20:26 NASB

Charles Smith, grandfather to four and great-grandfather to ten, always wore a smile on his face. He greeted everyone with a smile. He offered a friendly smile before parting with others. Charles even smiled when he talked on the telephone. Unbelievably, this smiling man came from what many people would consider a childhood of terror.

Charles, the oldest of five brothers, grew up poor in an abusive family in the early 1900s. His father, an alcoholic, beat his wife regularly. The boys lived in fear that he might kill her. One day when Charles and his brothers were in school, a tornado ripped through their town, killing two-thirds of their classmates. This abruptly ended their schooling. The tornado destroyed Charles' own home except for the wall that stood beside the stove, where his mother was cooking.

> Wrinkles appear where smiles have been.

All five of the Smith brothers lived during the Depression. They all served in the armed forces and contributed to service-oriented careers. Charles was the only one who came out smiling, however. One brother drank. Two of them physically abused their wives. The other one suffered with poor health.

Charles attributed his positive outlook to his godmother who took him to church each Sunday. It was his relationship with God that allowed him to keep his smile, even though he faced some of life's worst circumstances.

His only daughter recalled, "Every night before he went to bed, I saw my father kneel down next to his bed to say his prayers."

Two of his grandsons often speak of the times they shared their problems with their grand-father. He always smiled and encouraged them to talk to God about their problems. He declared that God is the "Man with the answers."

Charles' family agrees that a kneeling man is a cheerful man.

*A glad heart makes a cheerful countenance.*

PROVERBS 15:13 AMP

61

> Grandparents always know
> just what to say—even
> when it's nothing at all.

Scott was fortunate to grow up in a house three doors down from his grandparents' home. His grandparents were like a second set of parents to him. In many ways, Scott considered them wiser than his own parents. When Scott wanted to quit Boy Scouts, his mother left the decision up to him. His grandpa, however, told him that he would like to see him stick it out for the entire year. Scott learned that quitting is not always the answer and stayed with the troop for the remainder of the year.

Scott was disappointed when he didn't make the cut for the high school football team. His father promised to talk to the coach. But his grandfather told him a story from his own life when he didn't make the baseball team.

Scott understood that everybody couldn't be successful at everything. Instead of playing baseball, Scott took a photography class. Photography became his passion and his livelihood for forty years.

Scott had the desire to go to a college out of state. His parents were insistent that he should attend the local junior college. His wise grandmother, who rarely voiced an opinion, spoke up and said, "Let the boy go. He needs to experience life." Scott's parents took her advice and allowed him to go.

When Scott proudly showed his grandmother the engagement ring that he picked out for his bride-to-be, Grandma hugged him warmly. With tears in her eyes, she said, "Honey, I am so proud of you."

Love always shines through with a small ray of encouragement from a grandparent.

*Little children, let us not love in word or speech but in deed and in truth.*
1 JOHN 3:18 RSV

Some children were asked about their grandmas.

**Why do you love your Grandma?**

Grandma always lets me have candy when I visit.

Grandma lets me help her.

Grandma plays checkers with me, and I win almost every time.

Grandma makes Easter eggs with me.

Grandma lets me help her make pies and cookies. I get to taste some of the dough too.

Grandma takes me for walks and tells me about birds. She knows a lot about birds.

Grandma lets me sleep at her house sometimes.

> The grandchild's creed:
> To God, country, and Grandma be true!

What does your Grandma do?

> When my mom gets a haircut, she comes to my house.
> She shops.
> She takes her dog for lots of walks.
> She goes to the doctor.
> Grandma cooks a lot of food that's yummy.
> She takes care of Grandpa.
> She plants flowers.

What is your favorite thing to do with Grandma?

> Hug her.
> Spend the night at her house.
> Play with the toys she keeps just for me.
> Eat chocolate together.

Grandmas have a special place in a child's heart. It seems God created them to meet a need that only a grandmother can fill.

*A wife of noble character who can find?*
*Her children arise and call her blessed;*
*her husband also, and he praises her.*
PROVERBS 31:10,28

> # A grandparent's love comes straight from the heart.

A pastor related the story of a young, gay man who had contracted AIDS. When he told his parents about his illness, they responded in shock and horror. His parents refused to see him for fear they could contract the disease. They took his pictures off the walls and acted as though he was no longer a part of their lives.

This young man told his grandmother of his demise. She explained to him that although she did not agree with his lifestyle, she still loved him. She gave him a big, grandmotherly hug and kiss. She wanted him to know she was not afraid of contracting the disease.

As time went on, his thin, frail body began to fail. Faithfully his grandmother continued to pray for him and to remind him that the Savior wanted to take care of him. Near the end, the emaciated grandson moved into his grandmother's home. With the help of outside nurses, his faithful grandmother cared for him until the end.

In his last moments, the young man confided to his grandmother that the tender care that she gave him made him feel loved for the very first time in his life. Previously, he had never found the love for which he had desperately sought.

Before he died, however, he accepted the greatest love by asking Christ into his heart. He reached out to the Savior because his grandmother's love reached out to him in the darkest time of his life.

We each have the power to love someone into eternity. Let's use that power with our grandchildren!

*Above all, love each other deeply, because love covers over a multitude of sins.*
1 PETER 4:8

Some of the gifts Margaret received from her children and grandchildren have gathered dust while others hold eternal value.

After becoming a grandmother, Margaret gained self-control. She had bitten her tongue many times in an attempt not to tell her daughter how to discipline her children.

Each time Margaret held a new grandbaby, she learned more about gentleness.

Margaret learned what kindness and gratitude is all about when she was sick in bed for two weeks and her daughter-in-law ran errands, cooked meals, and fluffed pillows.

Margaret acquired patience every time one of her grandchildren entered the terrible twos!

> The riches stored in a grandparent's heart can never be stolen.

When her grandchildren spent the night with her, Margaret witnessed total peace as they were sleeping quietly. And Margaret reveled in joy while she watched a grandchild marvel at a first snowfall.

The most precious gift of all came to Margaret, however, when she watched a granddaughter die of leukemia. She felt that God had given her the gift of love as she endured this heartbreaking experience. God gave her enough love to comfort her son. She loved her granddaughter enough to be able to kiss her good-bye. She loved God enough to trust Him during the most difficult time in her life.

All of these experiences God had turned to gold in Margaret's heart. What kinds of eternal gifts has God placed in your life today?

*"Store up for yourselves treasures in heaven, where moth and rust do not destroy, and where thieves do not break in and steal. For where your treasure is, there your heart will be also."*

MATTHEW 6:20-21

> ## Keep pouring out
> ## kindness and love—
> ## God won't let them run dry.

It was only a few weeks before Christmas. World War I was in progress. Both sides of the warring trenches were filled with men. Some were young while others were old. Each one, however, was tired, dirty, and homesick.

Screams pierced the sound of the gun shells. Over and over, pitiful pleading could be heard. *"Hilf mir, hilf mir,"* a young German soldier cried. He was calling out for help. He was tangled up in barbwire and had been wounded by a bullet. A young American soldier couldn't take the cries of the enemy any longer. He crawled out of his trench and over to the moaning boy.

When his fellow fighters saw what was happening, they ceased their fire. The young

American soldier scooped the wounded man into his arms. He walked toward the German trenches carrying the wounded serviceman.

Immediately, the German soldiers stopped shooting as well. The American soldier gingerly handed the injured man to his fellow citizen. He turned to walk away. Suddenly, he felt the grip of a strong hand on his shoulder. He spun around to face a German officer holding something small in his hand. It was the Iron Cross, the highest metal for bravery a soldier can earn. The officer thrust the weighty piece into the brave young man's hand. The American soldier crawled back into the trenches, and the shooting resumed.

When God calls us to express a kindness for someone else, no matter the risk, there will always be a reward awaiting us.

Don't be afraid to step across the battleground of broken families to love your grandchildren.

*The righteous giveth and spareth not.*
PROVERBS 21:26 KJV

Lou Gehrig loved baseball. In high school, Lou was the star player on his ball team. After he graduated from college, a scout for the New York Yankees hired him to play professionally.

For the next fourteen years, Lou Gehrig played 2,130 consecutive games. The boy who never missed a day of grade school became the man who never missed a ball game. Lou played despite stomachaches, broken fingers, and back pain. His teammates called him, "Iron Horse." When asked how he did it, the shy and modest Lou explained by saying, "That's just the way I am."

> A good example is the best sermon.

In 1939, Lou was diagnosed with a deadly disease that affected his central nervous system. Lou never complained about his terrible illness.

Instead, in a speech he made to the Yankee audience, he said, "Fans, for the past two weeks, you have been reading about a bad break of mine. Yet today, I consider myself the luckiest man on the face of the earth."

Lou was offered many jobs after he retired from baseball. He chose to work for the Parole Commission. He believed that by filling that position, he might be able to do something for the city that loved him so much. Lou Gehrig died in 1941. At his funeral, the minister announced that there would be no speeches made. "We need none, because you all knew him." Lou Gehrig's way of living said it all.

Our lives will speak for us long after we are gone. To live as a reflection of Christ is the greatest legacy we can leave to the world— and to our grandchildren.

*He who walks with the wise grows wise.*
PROVERBS 13:20

## Be youthful—
## even if you're old
## everywhere else!

Neal and Nancy enjoyed spending time with their grandparents while their parents worked. Each morning, Grandpa waited in his bed on the sleeping porch until the kids arrived. Neal and Nancy would race from the car, run across the front porch, and fling open the screen door. They would make a beeline through the house to Grandpa's bed. After a great deal of giggling and tickling, a full-fledged pillow fight usually would erupt.

Grandma always was busy cooking breakfast when the kids arrived. She would smile even though Neal and Nancy wouldn't stop long enough to give her a hug. She knew that Grandpa's pillow fights were much more enticing than a sentimental kiss. She would stand back and let the fun begin.

As the ham and bacon sizzled, the biscuits in the oven would turn a golden brown. Finally, by the time the delightful aroma drifted through the house, Grandpa and the kids would make their way to the dining-room table and join Grandma for a delicious meal.

The gleeful morning hours started each day with happiness. Grandpa and Neal usually would retreat to the living room to quietly read the newspaper or to watch television after breakfast. Grandma and Nancy would clear off the table, wash the breakfast dishes, and put on the vegetables for lunch.

The children learned many valuable lessons from their grandparents as a result of those early morning visits. The greatest lesson they learned, however, was that love can be expressed with laughter, good food, quiet time spent together, and even early morning pillow fights. Love isn't simply spoken. It's lived.

*A happy heart is good medicine and*
*a cheerful mind works healing.*
PROVERBS 17:22 AMP

One of the greatest gifts grandparents can give their grandchildren is time. Parents don't always have the time to play games with their children. Grandparents can usually find the time to throw a ball, to bake muffins from scratch, or to go for a walk. They can find the time to teach their grandchildren to tie their shoes, ride a bike, or make peanut butter and jelly sandwiches.

Steve's grandparents went to every single ball game, soccer match, and Christmas program. He vividly remembers seeing them as they sat on the front row at church or in the high school gymnasium, cheering him on. His grandfather always wore one of his gray hats. Grandma usually arrived in a floral dress. They attended every graduation, meet-the-teacher day, and science fair. Steve reflected

> Because they loved them right from the start, kids love grandparents with all their hearts.

on the many times they shared ice cream together on Wednesday nights after church. He thought often about the Sunday lunches and the cold drinks after ball games on hot summer nights.

"My grandparents purchased gifts that I really wanted on my birthdays," Steve laughed. "They put a lot of thought into the gifts they bought. They didn't buy what they liked. They took the time to decide what a boy my age would like and purchased that special treasure regardless of the price."

After Steve married and his children came along, his life became very busy. Steve made it a priority to call his grandparents, however, on a weekly basis. They had willingly given him their time when he was a child, and he decided that he would give them some of his time after he became an adult.

Children and grandparents often spell love "T-I-M-E."

*Children are a gift from God;*
*they are his reward.*
PSALM 127:3 TLB

> # Love is a little word;
>
> # Grandmas make it big.

Grandma took her twin grandsons shopping at their favorite department store. When the boys spied a turnkey Superball machine on the sidewalk, they asked Grandma for a dime each. She rambled through her purse until she pulled out two shiny dimes.

Brad put his dime in, and out fell a Superball. Chad carefully dropped his dime into the slot, turned the key, and opened the latch. His ball fell out, hit the pavement, and started bouncing. He tried to catch it, but since the store was located on a hill, the ball quickly escaped.

Grandma saw what had happened, told the boys to stay put, and ran to catch the runaway Superball. She didn't think about what she was doing before she did it. She ran across the

78

parking lot, dodged shopping carts, and avoided several cars that were backing out of the parking places. People stopped and stared, at this grandmother chasing a tiny Superball.

She didn't let any obstacle stop her and continued to chase the ball until she caught it. When she returned to the curb where the boys were standing, she smiled as she handed Chad his runaway ball.

Loving grandparents do many sacrificial things for grandchildren without even thinking. They try to bring happiness to their lives at any expense. This grandma's love for her grandson was exemplified that day when she chased the Superball across a busy parking lot. Her grandchildren learned what God's love looked like as they watched her.

And when asked if she would do it again, she smiled and said, "In a heartbeat."

*All thy children shall be taught of the LORD;*
*and great shall be the peace of thy children.*
ISAIAH 54:13 KJV

When Willie Mae was a child, she loved to go fishing. Her grandmother always told her that there were certain things that a person shouldn't do on Sunday, out of respect for God. Unfortunately, fishing was one of those things. Willie Mae couldn't understand what on earth was wrong with fishing. It was fun, and if she caught any fish, they could eat them for dinner that night.

> A grandparent has silver hair, tin ears, a lead bottom, and a heart of gold.

One particular Sunday afternoon, Willie Mae was visiting with her grandmother. Knowing how her grandmother felt about fishing, Willie Mae crept to the barn, pulled out her fishing pole, and headed to the pond. Once she was far enough away from the house that she couldn't be seen, Willie Mae kicked up her heels and prayed that the fish would be biting.

She sat down on the bank and got comfortable. She baited her hook and threw the line into the water. About that time, Willie Mae heard an audible voice. "Are you fishing on Sunday?" She looked around and didn't see anyone. But suddenly, she heard that same voice again. "Are you fishing?"

"Nope. I'm not fishing!" Willie Mae exclaimed. She pulled in the line and ran as fast as she could back to her grandmother's house. For the remainder of her years, Willie Mae never had the desire to go fishing on Sunday again.

Some sixty years later, Willie Mae shared that story with her granddaughter. This simple story taught them both a great lesson: *if there's a doubt about whether a particular action is right or wrong—don't do it at all!*

*Gray hair is a crown of splendor;*
*it is attained by a righteous life.*

PROVERBS 16:31

## A Poem for Grandma

For the twinkle in Grandma's eyes,
For her tender lullabies,
For all the fun she has in store,
I'll love her always, plus one day more.

Carol Burnett, the famous comedienne, grew up with her mom, sister, and her beloved grandmother, Nanny. One Sunday morning, Carol's Sunday school class ended early. She became impatient as she waited for Nanny to come get her after the conclusion of the morning service. Carol was wearing a suit her grandmother had made for her, which included a blue felt hat with a big red feather sticking out of the top.

Carol made her way to the sanctuary and peeked through the double doors. She couldn't see Nanny.

*What if she has fainted?* Carol wondered. *What if she has died?* Not able to wait any longer, Carol got down on all fours and proceeded to crawl down the aisle, peering down each pew in search of her grandmother.

Since the pastor was speaking on the subject of love, Carol figured that God wouldn't mind her looking for her Nanny, if she did it in the quietest way possible. She was so intent on crawling that she didn't notice the church had gotten completely quiet.

Someone in the congregation finally broke the silence. "There is a little Indian here in our church." Everyone started to laugh.

Carol immediately caught a glimpse of her grandmother, flung herself into her arms, and started to cry. "Everyone is laughing at me, Nanny."

"No," Nanny wisely replied. "They're laughing at your feather."

With the words we use, we can heal and soften wounds. We can also calm and reassure a child.

*She opens her mouth in skillful*
*and godly Wisdom, and on her*
*tongue is the law of kindness.*
PROVERBS 31:26 AMP

Elizabeth Elliot, the well-known Christian author of *Shadow of the Almighty,* had a grandfather who touched American history. Frank Clemens Gillingham was an officer in the Union Army. President Lincoln's body was transported to Springfield, Illinois, after he was shot at Ford's Theatre. Elizabeth's grandfather was in charge of the funeral train. The train made a long, languorous push west, carrying the body of its beloved president. It stopped in each town it came to, so the residents would have the opportunity to pay their last respects to this fallen hero. Grandpa Gillingham remembered the trip vividly. It was his job at each stop to gently wipe the cinders from Lincoln's face.

During a lifetime, a person never knows what job they will be called to do. For a few,

## A Poem for Grandpa

He can pull a nickel
from his ear
And tickles me
when I get near.
Then he sets me
on his knee;
I love my grandpa,
and he loves me!

life will consist of fame and fortune as the president or as a beloved sports hero. For others, it will be a dramatic life ministering to the sick and dying of India. Or some people may be given the opportunity to reach out to lepers or AIDS victims.

Others of us may be called to reach out to the world by sending donations to starving children or even going to the mission field to help hands-on. We may be called to make a difference in our own communities by ministering to those at our own backdoors. We all have jobs to do and positions to fill. We can all be grandparents that our grandchildren call blessed.

We may not always remember everything we do, but our grandchildren will always remember the things that made them proud of us. Because those memories will profoundly affect their lives, let us never hesitate to do what is good.

*Do not withhold good*
*from those who deserve it,*
*when it is in your power to act.*
PROVERBS 3:27

# God is never further
# than a prayer away.

Once the breakfast dishes were done, the grandmother sat down at the dining room table. Her eight-year-old granddaughter, Nancy, worried about why she sat in a dark room looking out the window.

"Are you sad, Grandma?" Nancy asked.

"No, honey, I'm not," Grandma responded. "I'm very happy."

It just didn't make sense to Nancy that someone could be happy not watching television, playing chase, or skipping rope. So Nancy continued to worry.

The next day, Grandma finished up with the breakfast dishes, sat down at the table, and stared outside again.

"Are you sure that you're not sad?" Nancy asked again.

"I'm sure, honey. Now run and play," Grandma responded.

When Nancy entered her teen years, her grandfather passed away. Before long, Grandma was forced to move away from the home that they had shared together. At times, Nancy wondered where Grandma sat when she wanted to be quiet.

Grandma passed away when Nancy was a young woman in her mid-twenties. Nancy missed her greatly but still couldn't understand Grandma's time at the window. Nancy loved playing games with her children and watching late night television.

After Nancy's children moved away, she better understood Grandma's need for her quiet time. The day after her son announced that he was going to be a father, Nancy sat quietly at her dining room table. She prayed for her grandchild that was on the way.

Suddenly, it dawned on Nancy why Grandma had sat quietly at her table each morning. She was praying for her grandchildren.

*Pray in the Spirit on all occasions with all kinds of prayers and requests.*
EPHESIANS 6:18

At the time that eleven-year-old Brian met his future running coach, Kane, he was living in a broken home. Kane was a man in his late fifties, trying to recover from a smothering divorce. Brian's mom was barely meeting the monthly bills. Kane found himself in the same situation. In an attempt to help each other out financially, Kane moved into the basement of Brian's home.

Month after month, year after year, Kane coached Brian in running. His trademark words were "hammer it home." At the end of a race, exhaustion can sometimes be overwhelming. But regardless, Kane encouraged Brian to "hammer it home."

> A grandparent teaches grandchildren to persevere cheerfully.

Over the years, Brian became lean and trim. His long muscles enabled him to have a confident running stride.

Kane, on the other hand, experienced severe muscle weakness. He suffered from Lou Gehrig's disease, but he "hammered it home" and continued to coach Brian from his wheelchair.

In Kane's final years, Brian and his mother took care of him. Kane taught Brian the principle of persevering or "hammering" even when it wasn't easy.

On June 6, Brian became the winner of the New Jersey State Meet of Champions. Seventeen days later, Kane died.

Perseverance is about caring for a loved one even when you are dealing with your own difficulties. It's also about encouraging and mentoring a young person whose hope is almost gone. And when hope seems lost, perseverance teaches praying, believing, and continuing on.

*I am hard-pressed from both directions,*
*having the desire to depart and be with*
*Christ, for that is very much better;*
*yet to remain on in the flesh is*
*more necessary for your sake.*

PHILIPPIANS 1:23-24 NASB

> We make a living by what
> we get, but we make
> a life by what we give.

Every Day is a Gift from Above. These words are printed beneath a photograph that was taken of a hammock hanging between two palm trees in the Bahamas.

Robert Benge snapped the picture on the last vacation his entire family took together. He was a man who adored his family and worked hard his entire lifetime. It was his desire that his children and grandchildren would have all of the things that he didn't have when he was growing up.

He and his wife, Grace, financed the entire trip to the Bahamas. They paid for the airline tickets, bus rides, and the cruise in its entirety for eleven people.

Robert gave his family many things over the years. The best treasure that he gave to them, however, was the ability to appreciate each and every day to its fullest. To Benge, life was a celebration and a gift from above. Because of the way they observed him daily living that appreciation, his family couldn't fail to learn the lesson.

When a person leaves this world, they usually leave something behind. Sometimes it may be fame or fortune. When Robert left this world, he left a sense of appreciation, love for each day, and the hope for eternity for his children and grandchildren.

What legacy will you leave for your family?

*Whatever is true, whatever is noble,*
*whatever is right, whatever is pure,*
*whatever is lovely, whatever is admirable—*
*if anything is excellent or praiseworthy—*
*think about such things.*

PHILIPPIANS 4:8

Grandpa didn't have a great deal of money, but he had a big heart. When the grandkids came for a visit, he almost always pulled out a dime apiece and sent them to the corner drugstore. The soda fountain there was a kid's dream come true. The kids could choose between numerous flavors, such as vanilla, chocolate, strawberry, and even butter pecan.

**Memories, not money, make you rich!**

When the grandkids opened a lemonade stand, Grandpa and Grandma were the first customers to arrive on the scene. Not only did they pay the required nickel for the cup of watered-down juice, they included an extra nickel for a tip.

Grandpa had lived through the Depression and was tight with his money, but he spent it willingly when it came to his grandchildren.

He showed a tremendous amount of love as he pulled the ten-cent pieces from his pocket for either an ice cream cone or a cup of lemonade. When his grandchildren were a little older, they realized that Grandpa did without extra things for himself so that he could provide special treats for them.

Today, when the grandchildren stop to consider the love that this man showed them when they were young, they feel very blessed. He loved without limits and gave with an open heart.

When we call on God, He does the same for us. He not only gives us the things we need, He also gives us many of the things we want.

*"Be on your guard against all kinds of greed; a man's life does not consist in the abundance of his possessions."*
LUKE 12:15

> # The greatest inheritance you can give your grandchildren is your faith.

A single mother wrote a list of instructions to her mother who was keeping her two boys for a few weeks. Once she had completed the instructions about their bedtimes and food preferences, she followed with this personal note: "And Mom, if you have the time, could you read the Bible and pray with the boys? This is something I never have time for."

The grandmother took this plea to heart. She devised a plan. She decided that the boys were probably used to taking a nap at a particular time each day, so she would institute a certain time to read the Bible. Each morning before snack time, they read the Bible together.

Knowing how much children love music, Grandma invested in some inexpensive praise tapes. She and the boys usually began their Bible time in a fun way by singing silly praise songs. Grandma didn't use her King James Version when she read to the boys. She took the children's Bible and read the words written on their level.

She also introduced them to Christian videotapes and coloring books. She borrowed materials from the children's Sunday school classroom. Grandma even used the stuffed animals that they brought along to explain about Noah and the ark.

When the boys returned home, they shared with their mom what they had learned. They told her stories about Daniel in the lions' den, David and Goliath, Noah and the ark, and all about Jesus Christ.

Grandparents have such a strong influence in the lives of their grandchildren. What seeds are you planting in yours?

*Preach the word; be ready*
*in season and out of season.*
2 TIMOTHY 4:2 NASB

Grandpa was a very smart man. He worked on a farm his entire lifetime, but eventually it came time for him to retire. He may have retired from his work, but he never slowed down. He continued to plant his garden year after year.

One year, Grandpa had a particularly hard time with small animals making themselves at home in his garden. They enjoyed munching on the delicacies that were growing in the garden. During the day, the scarecrow kept the critters away, but at night, they slipped in to steal Grandpa's produce.

> In youth, we learn. In age, we understand.

Grandpa became frustrated. He ran an extension cord to the garden and turned on the radio. This worked well for a couple of nights. Once the critters became accustomed to the music, however, they went back to munching on the garden delicacies. Grandpa, being the wise man he was, began contemplating other ways to keep the critters away. And he prayed out of desperation.

While pulling his hoe from the storage house one day, he spied a Santa Claus standing diligently in the corner. Alas, an idea was born. He pulled old Saint Nick out, dusted him off, and stood him in the field, even though it was the middle of July. At night, Grandpa lit him up.

Santa performed two jobs well. He kept the critters away. He also let the grandkids know what Santa does with his time during the summer months.

As we grow older, God gives us better insights into ways to improve our lives using the wisdom that He gives to us.

*If any of you lacks wisdom, he should ask God, who gives generously to all.*

JAMES 1:5

GLDB

## Godly grandparents
## make life grand.

A grandmother explained Heaven to her grandson Austin. She told him about the golden streets and the light that shines from God's throne. She described the Lamb's Book of Life. She told him how it contains all the names of those who have received Jesus into their hearts.

"When you, your mommy, your daddy, and your brother all go to Heaven, an angel with white feathery wings will open up the big book. She will call for your daddy, and he will say, 'Here.'

"Then the angel will read your mommy's name, and she will say, 'Here.' Then the angel will call your brother's name, and he will say, 'Here.' And then the angel will call your name and you will say, . . .'"

The dark-headed boy paused for a few seconds.

"Grandma," he finally replied, "I'll say 'Here,' but I better yell real loud just in case the angel doesn't see me."

Later that week, the unthinkable happened. A car struck Austin. Unfortunately, Austin was bleeding internally as a result of the injury. He could not be saved.

His grieving family crowded around his hospital bed. They witnessed his long eyelashes flutter as the end drew near. Finally, it seemed that Austin was trying to sit up. Very softly, he uttered, "Here," and he was gone.

Children need someone to paint a picture repeatedly of who God is, so they can carry it for the rest of their lives. Grandparents are magnificent artists.

*"Blessed are those who wash their robes,*
*that they may have the right to the tree of life*
*and may go through the gates into the city."*
REVELATION 22:14

When Agnes Bojaxhiu became a nun at age eighteen, no one knew the tremendous impact she would have on the world. In 1937, she took her final vows and adopted the new name of "Teresa." She was later known as Mother Teresa.

In 1948, Mother Teresa set aside her stiff collar and formal robe. She adopted a simple white cotton sari, the dress of the poor women of India. She formed a ministry called the Missionaries of Charity.

Mother Teresa and the other nuns who joined her took care of India's unlovely—the poorest of the poor. They assisted people who were dying on the streets and the abandoned children. She and her sisters took care of them, regardless of their faith.

**The heart that loves is always young.**

Over the next few years, Mother Teresa opened new missionary houses in Venezuela, Italy, Australia, England, and the United States. Eventually, she was awarded the Nobel Peace Prize for her great work.

Mother Teresa's life was one of constant struggle, but she carried on gladly, even in old age. The Indian poet Rabindranath Tagore once wrote about her:

I slept and dreamt that life was joy
I awoke and saw that life was duty
I acted and behold duty was joy.

We may not all have the opportunity to travel to India, but we can love the poor citizens who live near us. Like Mother Teresa, we can discover that our duties will also become our joy. As grandparents, we can pass this joy to our grandchildren, who will in turn pass it on to their children.

*Many waters cannot quench love,*
*neither can floods drown it.*
Song of Solomon 8:7 RSV

The most important thing a grandpa
can do for his grandchildren
is to love their grandma.

In February 1922, the very first issue of *Reader's Digest* hit the newsstands. DeWitt Wallace had the idea to put together a magazine of condensed articles. In 1910, he enthusiastically sent out samples to many different publishers. Unfortunately, not one editor was interested in DeWitt's plan for a new publication. He became very discouraged when he received one rejection after another. He almost gave up on the idea.

Shortly afterward, DeWitt met a beautiful young woman named Lila Bell Acheson. They were married in October 1921. Lila listened intently as DeWitt shared his idea for the magazine with her. She thought it was a great idea. She encouraged DeWitt not to give up on his literary goal. She helped him make his dream come true.

People soon began hearing about the publication and requested their own subscriptions. Before long DeWitt and Lila were very busy managing their own magazine. They worked at it together. DeWitt considered Lila his cofounder, coeditor, and co-owner.

Today, *Readers Digest* is the best-selling magazine in the entire world, printed in eighteen different languages. DeWitt once made this statement: "I think Lila made the *Digest* possible."

When you love someone as you love yourself, you have the potential to help that person achieve God's potential for his or her life. For love believes all things, hopes all things, endures all things (1 Corinthians 13:7 NASB). Love also has a way of making dreams come true. How can you help make your spouse's dreams come true?

*So ought men to love their wives as their own bodies. He that loveth his wife loveth himself.*
EPHESIANS 5:28 KJV

Harold and Charlotte were in their sixties when they made the decision to move from Ontario to New York City, where they had grown up as children. They were a bit nervous moving into a higher crime area, but were delighted to be near old friends and family once again.

One night they heard a knock at the door. Harold carefully opened the steel reinforced door. "May I help you?" he asked.

"Checking the lights," was the quick reply.

"We didn't ask for our lights to be checked," Harold replied and firmly closed the door.

He sat down by his wife chuckling.

"This guy probably thinks he can fool an older man," Harold said. "I might be older than him, but he will find out that I'm smarter too."

> Humor goes a long way toward easing the bumps in the road of life.

Suddenly, there was an even louder knock at the door.

"Checking the lights," the mystery man shouted.

"If you don't leave, I'll call the police," Harold yelled back.

About that time, the phone rang. It was the neighbor from next door.

"Did I hear someone knocking at your door?" he asked.

"Yes," Charlotte replied, "it's someone who wants to check our lights."

The neighbor started to laugh. "No, I think that must be the guy from Chicken Delight with our dinner."

With God's help, we can adjust to new addresses, new jobs, new homes, new neighbors, and new life environments. Our circumstances in life may change, but we can find strength in knowing that God never changes.

*Everlasting joy will be theirs.*
ISAIAH 61:7

> The only joy greater than seeing
> your grandchildren is seeing
> your great-grandchildren!

Mama was beaming when her great-grand-sons came into the world. She was delighted to have become a great-grandmother. But she was even more elated when she discovered that the family had been doubly blessed with identical twin boys.

When Mama was asked to help out for a couple of weeks, she eagerly accepted. Mama didn't mind the loads of diapers that she folded. She actually enjoyed sitting up at night rocking the babies one at a time. Mama sang lullabies as she helped to prepare dozens of bottles each morning.

The following weekend, everyone gathered together to get to know the newest members of the family. Mama got up early that morning. She dressed in her finest purple pantsuit. She washed and styled her hair. She wanted to have her picture made with the boys.

She was so proud of the twins, and she wanted to send photos to her sister and her friends who lived out of state.

Many times that day, cameras flashed. Mama smiled brightly in most all of the pictures, even though the boys slept.

Traditionally, Mama ran away from a camera. On that day, however, she found her way into almost every photograph that was taken. And in every picture, she was smiling from ear to ear. The joy in her heart was obvious by the expression on her face.

When God allows a mother to live long enough to become a great-grandmother, He has given her a picture-perfect gift.

*That you, and your children and their children after them may fear the LORD your God as long as you live by keeping all his decrees and commands that I give you, and so that you may enjoy long life.*

DEUTERONOMY 6:2

A grandmother and her fourteen-month-old granddaughter were spending the afternoon together. Nana picked up the baby and a recent photograph album. "Look, here's Hannah," Nana declared. And here's Hannah, and here's Hannah." Hannah stared at the pictures.

"Here is Aunt Becky and Brian. Look, there's Uncle Brad and Amy too," Nana further announced. "Here's a picture of Mommy and Daddy!" Hannah's eyes were glued to the photo album. Nana flipped to the next page. Amazing as it was, there was a picture of the photographer herself, Nana. "Someone must have stolen the camera," Nana reasoned.

When Hannah spied the picture of Nana, she looked up into her grandmother's eyes. She

> You find so many reasons to smile once you become a grandparent.

smiled a little sly smile, crinkled her nose, and then grinned. It warmed Nana's heart to know that Hannah recognized her in the picture.

God gave us a beautiful world. Many times as we go about our daily living, we recognize God in the things we see, feel, and hear. We can see His eyes in the sunrise. As the wind blows, we can feel His tender touch. At the sound of ocean waves, God's power is revealed. When we look toward the heavens in gratitude and smile up at God, it warms His heart, as well.

Recognizing God in all things is easy—for God is the beginning and the end, the first and the last, and everything in between. And God loves it when His children take the time to notice all the good things that He has done for them.

*"I am the Alpha and the Omega,"*
*says the Lord God.*
REVELATION 1:8

Being a grandparent can feel like a marathon—you need perseverance and good, comfortable shoes.

Two grandmas were reminiscing over cups of steaming coffee. They were discussing the joys of being grandparents. Quickly the conversation was converted to the struggles they faced with aging.

"I've discovered that as my family expands with grandchildren, sons-in-law, and daughters-in-law, that life is speeding by," Grace confessed. "It is almost like I am in a race against time."

"I understand that," Elizabeth agreed. "And it takes longer to get even my routine tasks done with this painful arthritis. I just seem to stumble through life at a slower speed while time flies quickly by me."

Grace took a swallow of coffee, laughed, and shook her head. "And I thought that with modern technology's implants, orthodontics, braces, dentures, plugs, screws, and hip replacements, I would be the bionic woman by now!"

Life is not always easy. It is true that the longer we live, the faster time flies and the slower we get. We can let the frustrations of life get us down, or we can make the best of them, enjoying every day that God has given to us.

The way we approach the difficulties in life says a great deal about our character. Laughing at our own infirmities has a way of lifting the heavy burdens from our shoulders. God can take our pain, hardships, and fears and turn them into something beautiful.

*Let us run with perseverance*
*the race marked out for us.*
HEBREWS 12:1

A man and his granddaughter were swimming in a pool one Sunday afternoon while Grandma watched. The water was over the little girl's head. Since she had a fear of water, she was afraid of going down the sliding board. But as afraid as she was, she wanted to give it a try.

"Will you catch me, Grandpa?" she shouted. Her grandfather agreed.

She walked to the ladder, climbed up, and down she went. Grandpa stood at the spot where she went under the water. He pulled her up, with a smile on his face, thinking that he had done his job well. His granddaughter wasn't smiling, however. She was coughing and crying.

"What's wrong, honey?" Grandpa asked.

> Having grandchildren doubles joy and divides grief in half.

"I thought you were going to catch me Grandpa!" she exclaimed, between coughs.

"Didn't you at least want to go under for a second?" he asked.

"No, Grandpa!" she cried. "I wanted you to catch me before I went under!"

As grandparents, we should be present to catch our grandchildren when they step out on a limb or attempt a feat in which they feel uncertain. Before we try to catch them, however, we need to understand at what point they would like for us to be there for them.

Some children may be the independent type. They may want to do things on their own. Others, however, may be like the little girl who wanted a helping hand even before she hit the water.

*All the ways of the LORD*
*are loving and faithful.*
PSALM 25:10

> Marriage has its low notes and high notes, but all in all, it's one sweet song, especially in the golden years.

The book *Shadowlands* tells the story of the late-in-life romance of English writer C.S. Lewis with Joy Gresham. When the couple first met, Lewis was a respected academic don at Oxford. Joy Gresham came to England for a visit and met Lewis at a church meeting. She was already an avid admirer of Lewis' writings. Soon a wonderful friendship began.

Over time, Lewis discovered that he had fallen deeply and unexpectedly in love with the vivacious brunette. Their courtship had its own wonderful quirkiness that came from a shy and intellectual Englishman dating a bold and outspoken American woman.

Lewis married Joy in name only to avoid her being deported from England. But after

Joy discovered that she had cancer, Lewis took her to his home to be his legal wife.

After a while, Joy's cancer went into remission. They enjoyed a few carefree years together as a married couple. When the cancer returned, they had to face the fact that they would not live happily ever after. After Joy's death, Lewis grappled with his trust in God.[1]

Years later, Lewis surmised, "Why love, if losing hurts so much? The pain is part of the happiness, then. That's the deal."[2]

We sometimes learn to appreciate the good things in life as a result of the bad. We were never guaranteed a perfect life, but we do know a perfect God, who sees the big picture and promises to comfort us when we walk through difficult times.

*I will betroth you to me forever; I will betroth you in righteousness and justice, in love and compassion.*

HOSEA 2:19

Lee Pitts wrote an article for his grandchildren several years ago. While grandparents want the best for their grandchildren, they are wise enough to understand that sometimes adversity teaches even greater and more valuable lessons. Here is an excerpt.

> I hope you don't always get brand new toys.

> I hope you fall a few times when you are learning to roller skate, so you learn that sometimes life is hard, even for a kid.

> I hope you break something big and expensive so your parents can tell you, "It's okay. We love you more than things." Then, I hope you have to do many jobs around the house to pay for the thing that isn't as important as you are.

**The invariable mark of wisdom is to see and hear the miraculous in the common.**

I hope one day your mom forgets to pick you up and you have to walk home, in the rain, on a windy day, so you can appreciate cars and the moms who drive them.

I hope someone threatens to beat up your sister and you step in to save her, even if you have to take a few punches.

I hope you learn to say thank-you from the heart.

I hope you learn to value people and not material goods.

I hope you always remember me.[3]

God desires to give us wisdom in this life. All He needs is a willing student.

*Let the wise listen.*

PROVERBS 1:5

> Work as if you were to live
> a hundred years; pray as if
> you were to die tomorrow.

Together, a family made an important decision. The father would leave his secular job and take a ministerial position. Every member of the family was willing to make the sacrifices needed to serve the Lord. This decision required a pay cut and a great deal of travel time.

As the years went by, the financial issues became more and more difficult. One night during the family prayer time, the youngest boy, Timmy, asked his father a question. "Do you think it would it be OK if I asked God for a new shirt?"

"Sure, son," was the father's reply. "I'm sure God can meet that need for you."

The father listed the request in the family prayer journal. Each night, Timmy made sure the family prayed about the shirt that he wanted so desperately.

A few weeks later, a Christian storeowner called Timmy's mother and told her that his store's summer sale was over. He explained that he had some boys shirts left over and wondered if she would be interested in them.

"Yes," she quickly replied. She thought about Timmy and his prayer request. "What size do you have?"

"Size seven," he answered. "By the way, I have twelve shirts left in that size."

That night during the family prayer time, Timmy received a dozen shirts that fit him perfectly. Timmy and his entire family learned a valuable lesson. And when they tell Tim's grandkids that story, that lesson is passed down: God meets our every need, answers every prayer, and usually goes beyond the expected to give us more.

*Cast your cares on the LORD*
*and he will sustain you;*
*he will never let the righteous fall.*

PSALM 55:22

The doorbell rang. Helen opened the door to an old man with an unkempt beard, dressed in scruffy clothing and shabby shoes. He had a wide grin and a southern drawl. His eyes were glazed over.

"Howdy do this morning," was his greeting. "Could I interest you kind folks in some vegetables from my garden?"

Helen peered inside his straw basket. She saw a few home-grown cucumbers, a head of lettuce, and tomatoes from his garden. Helen felt sorry for the man and bought some of the cucumbers from his basket. She hoped that would be the last time she would see him.

Every Saturday morning, however, the man returned. Occasionally, he brought along a song with him. On a weekly basis, he knocked

> As the purse is emptied, the heart is filled.

on the door, holding a basket full of produce. As Helen's family got to know Sandy, they discovered the glaze in his eyes was from cataracts, not liquor. And surprisingly, he was not homeless. He lived just down the street from them in an old broken-down shack.

One morning Sandy greeted Helen and her husband, John, with an extra bounce in his step.

"You'll never believe what I found outside my door yesterday!" he exclaimed. "Somebody left a sack full of men's shoes!"

"Wow, that's great," John said. "I bet you're feeling really blessed."

"Oh, yes I am," Sandy continued excitedly. "I even found someone who could use them!"

Whether it is the widow's mite or a large check, God sees how we give, how often we give, and how much we give.

The whole family learned something about a giving heart from Sandy that day.

*God loves a cheerful giver.*
2 CORINTHIANS 9:7

> # Grandparents can always be at their best, regardless of age.

Grandma Sheridan had lost some of her mental capabilities. She was as sweet as ever and tried to be helpful, but her memory was not as clear as it once had been. The one memory that stuck with her, however, was the written Word—the Holy Bible. Grandma remembered a verse for almost every occasion. Her favorite verse was Matthew 22:37, "Love the Lord your God with all your heart and with all your soul and with all your mind."

But as time went on, even the scriptures started to slip from her mind. "Love the Lord with your mind, or was soul first?" Many times she got the order of words mixed up and confused. When that happened, she hurried over to pick up her Bible to look them up to refresh her memory. At the end of her life, she resided in a Christian nursing home. She was placed on complete bed rest.

The day she went to Heaven, she couldn't speak above a whisper. It was very hard for the family to understand what she was trying to say.

Finally her daughter leaned over her bed and listened carefully. "Mom, what are you trying to say?"

Grandma's eyes fluttered open for a brief second. "Love," she whispered. She was quoting what she could remember of her favorite Scripture verse. And at that moment the entire family realized that one word truly summed up the entire Gospel: *love.*

Even on our deathbeds, we can share the most important truth we will ever experience in life: *love.*

*Those who have served well
gain an excellent standing.*
1 TIMOTHY 3:13

When their daughter, Hannah, was born, Lucy and Chad were generous. Even though they loved Hannah with all their hearts and wanted to spend a great deal of time with her, they knew that Hannah needed to have a close relationship with all of her grandparents. The proud parents invited everyone to their house for dinner a few days after they returned home from the hospital.

> **Surrounded by grandparents—surrounded by love!**

When Hannah was just a couple of months old, the couple left her in the care of her Nana and Pa. They went out of town for a couple of nights. The young family lived several hours away; therefore when Hannah went to visit with her grandparents, she stayed for several days at a time.

Hannah was a fortunate little girl to have so many grandparents who loved her dearly.

Each grandparent was thrilled, too, to have the opportunity to spend time with her on a regular basis. They were all thankful for Lucy and Chad's generosity.

Whether Hannah is with her Nana and Pa, her Nannie and Papa, Maw Maw and Paw Paw, or with Grandma and Grandpa, she receives numerous hugs and kisses with every visit. Hannah receives a special gift each time she visits with a grandparent. All of her grandparents feel that having time to spend with Hannah is a wonderful present as well. When it comes to grandparents, the more a child has, the merrier she will be. There's no such thing as too many grandparents.

Are you one of many grandparents? Never feel that you are one too many. Enjoy your grandchildren. You are the only grandparent like you that they have.

*He will quiet you with his love,*
*he will rejoice over you with singing.*
ZEPHANIAH 3:17

One advantage of a bad memory
is that you can repeatedly
enjoy the same joke.

It had gotten hard to talk to Grandpa. His eyesight was failing, and his hearing aids didn't always work. But he managed to overcome these challenges and turn his visits into fun events. He always had gum and candy in his pockets; and if shouting the request didn't work for a grandchild, a pat on the arm and pointing at the pocket did.

The little ones enjoyed the game he invented in which they would write secret messages in big print to him, which he told them had to be big "to fool the mice."

Sitting beside Grandpa on a porch swing was a wonderful time of peace, and the warmth of his love always came through when he patted a shoulder or his voice boomed, "Ah, the Lord is good!"

The older grandchildren worked out a fast system of communicating with Grandpa with a large computer screen and a word processing program. Grandpa learned to use his computer to "chat" with them each day. Grandpa knew the secret of rising above challenges, and he lived it cheerfully before his grandchildren.

As we grow older, interacting with others may become a challenge. Always remember that if you love your grandchildren, they will know it and work with you through those challenges. Come up with creative ways to relate in spite of any hearing or vision losses. Small treats and tender messages go a long way toward smoothing the sometimes-interrupted lines of communication. And don't be afraid to get technological to stay in touch. Your grandchildren are worth your effort.

*Be patient with each other, making allowance for each other's faults because of your love.*
EPHESIANS 4:2 TLB

Bob Hope is one of America's favorite entertainers. His theater performances, radio broadcasts, movie and television appearances, and his personal entertainment shows landed him a spot in the *Guinness Book of World Records* as the most honored entertainer.

Bob has had an unwavering commitment in supporting the morale of America's servicemen. He has traveled to England, Africa, Ireland, Italy, Beirut, the South Pacific, Germany, Vietnam, and the Persian Gulf to entertain the troops. The service members soon dubbed him "GI Bob." In 1997, he became an honorary veteran.

> A couple can accomplish much if they don't care which partner gets the credit.

For over sixty of these years, he has had a woman by his side. Dolores Reade was a young singer when Bob met her. They were married in February, 1934. Dolores toured with Bob on all of the major stages until she paused her musical career to sing lullabies to their four children.

In the late 40s, she returned to the stage to help Bob entertain the troops all over the world. And in 1990, she and Bob were in Saudi Arabia to entertain the troops. A few years later, Bob stood by her side as she christened the USS *Bob Hope,* a navy vessel.

Dolores has spent her entire life supporting Bob and their children. In 1993, after Bob's persistent encouragement, she recorded her first CD. "I wish she would get steady work," quips Bob.

Bob and Dolores Hope have learned that giving support and encouragement is part of loving each other. Along those lines, Nancy Reagan once said, "Marriage is not 50-50; it's each of you giving 100 percent." The Hopes understand that secret to a happy marriage.

*Do nothing from selfishness or empty conceit, but with humility of mind regard one another as more important than yourselves.*

PHILIPPIANS 2:3 NASB

GLDB

> # Move out in faith, and you will find the hoped-for promises of God.

One afternoon, an old man was resting on his front porch. His granddaughter joined him. It wasn't long before a dusty car pulled up. A lanky man stepped out to stretch for a few seconds.

While scratching his head, he asked, "What kind of town is this?"

The old man wisely replied, "Well, what kind of town did you come from?"

"I come from a town where people don't help each other. No one is very neighborly," answered the young man.

"That is exactly what you will find here," warned the old man.

About an hour later, another car pulled up. Out tumbled three boys hopping up and down. A slightly rumpled young mother politely asked, "Could my boys use your restroom?" The old man obliged.

As she waited for them, she asked, "What kind of town is this?"

The old man wisely replied," Well, what kind of town did you come from?"

"Oh," she answered, "it's a wonderful place to live. Everyone helps and shares with those in need."

The old man nodded and smiled. "That's exactly what this town is like."

When the mother and her children drove off, the man's granddaughter asked, "Why did you give two different descriptions of our town?"

"Because, my dear," he explained, "what your town is like is determined by what kind of person you are."

Teach your grandchildren that it doesn't matter what you give—whether it's a smile, money, or time—what you give is what you will get in return.

*"Give, and it will be given to you.*
*A good measure, pressed down, shaken*
*together and running over, will be poured*
*into your lap. For with the measure*
*you use, it will be measured to you."*

LUKE 6:38

A wife woke up early one morning with something on her heart. She realized she was living in a miserable marriage. For a few minutes, she prayed, asking God to release her from the agonizing marriage. God spoke to her that morning.

"Lord, should I pray for my husband, even though he is not praying for me?"

*"Yes,"* was the Lord's prompt reply.

"You see how he acts, God," she complained.

The Lord noted, *"Have you noticed the way you have acted lately?"*

"Lord, are You asking me to change?"

> If you would have God hear you when you pray, you must hear Him when He speaks.

*"Yes, my child. Are you ready to know how to make that change?"*

"I suppose so God. But I still think that he is the one who needs to change."

*"My dear, it's not about who needs to change, but who is willing to let Me change them."*

"But God," the wife persisted, "this doesn't seem fair."

*"You are right. Life is not always fair. But remember, I am always just."*

"OK Lord, but You have got to help me have a good attitude about this."

*"Your attitude is what* you *decide to make it."*

"Go ahead and change me, Lord."

*"Now you are ready to pray for your husband."*

If we want to change others, we must first allow God to change us from the inside out. Once we are changed, we should forgive, show understanding, and offer grace to everyone. That is God's way, and it should be our way too!

*May your fountain be blessed, and may you rejoice in the wife of your youth.*
PROVERBS 5:18

GLDB

## Life is fragile—
## handle with prayer.

Every occurrence in a child's life is worthy of prayer. First ball games, dance recitals, and first dates are events worthy of prayer. Another event that calls for prayer is the birth of the first grandchild.

Dear Lord,

Bless this little life that you just placed in my arms. It's hard to believe that I'm a grandmother. It seems like just yesterday when you placed my own babies in my arms. She's adorable, Lord. She's Daddy's precious little girl and Mama's little angel. But she has stolen Nana's heart. I'll never be the same again.

Bless her Lord. Teach her to love your creatures of the wild. Give her the hope she needs to get through every day and the courage to become the person that you would have her to be when she grows up.

Stay close to her and send your angels to guard and protect her. And please let her always know that her grandmother loves her more than she loves life itself. She's a very special delivery Lord, and I ask your every blessing on her.[4]

As years quickly pass, the grandmother will look back with fond remembrance, knowing that her prayers made a difference in the lives of her children and grandchildren.

*Be joyful always; pray continually;*
*give thanks in all circumstances.*
1 THESSALONIANS 5:16

When a lady in her seventies started showing signs of a possible stroke, her concerned family took her to the doctor. Immediately following the examination, the doctor sent her to the hospital to have a CAT scan.

The grandmother, her daughter, and her grandson were nervously sitting in the bleak waiting room. For a few minutes, there were no words spoken. Her seven-year-old grandson picked up a magazine and started flipping through it. Suddenly, he laughed aloud at one cartoon in particular.

**Grandparents and grandchildren make each other laugh!**

"Here, Grandma," he said, as he handed her the ripped-out page. "When they ask you what you're here for, just give them this cartoon."

The silver-haired grandma looked at the picture and started to grin. It was a drawing of a doctor waving a cat over a woman lying on an examining table, saying, "This won't hurt a bit, I am just going to give you a cat scan!" The air in the room became much lighter, as the three generations began to laugh together.

There are seasons in our lives when it is hard to find something to laugh about. But even in our old age, laughter is still the best medicine, and joy is always on our side. God loves for us to laugh in the face of adversity and smile when we feel more like crying. When we laugh, we are expressing faith in His promise to care for us. And if we're able to laugh, life doesn't seem quite so difficult.

*Be joyful always.*
1 THESSALONIANS 5:16

GLDB

> Money can't buy health,
> happiness, or what it
> bought last year.

A young boy shopping in a store just before Christmas saw an amazing sight. He spied a crisp one hundred dollar bill face down on the floor. He excitedly scooped it up and rushed over to his grandmother.

"Grandma, look what I found," he whispered loudly.

The wise grandmother saw this as an opportunity to teach her grandson a lesson. "You can't keep it honey," she explained

"What?" he said incredulously. "But I- I found it. Finders keepers, losers weepers."

"I'm sorry, son, but that money belongs to someone else. The right thing to do is to turn it in. The person might come back looking for it." She and the disappointed boy trudged over to the customer service desk and explained the situation.

The clerk behind the counter dutifully took the boy's name and number. She explained that they would hold the money and call him if nobody claimed it within the month.

A week later the phone rang. Sure enough, a lady had lost the money and came back looking for it. She was calling to thank the young boy for his integrity.

"It was the only money I had for Christmas. My children wouldn't have received a single present if it hadn't been for your honesty."

When the boy told his grandmother about the call, he was grinning inside and out.

The lesson this young man learned from his grandmother was worth more than any amount of money.

*Wealth is worthless in the day of wrath,*
*but righteousness delivers from death.*
PROVERBS 11:4

A couple adopted a five-year-old boy from Korea. They named him Garrett. When Garrett arrived in the United States, he immediately became this *perfect* child. He couldn't do enough to please his new parents. Garrett was obedient to the letter of the law, although he knew no English and the parents didn't speak a word of Korean. The parents assumed this extreme obedience was part of his culture.

> Train up children in the way they should go, and walk there yourself once in a while.

A few weeks after Garrett had become part of the family, his parents went to a church conference. They were excited to take Garrett, because a Korean woman would be attending. Now was their chance to ask their son some important questions, and for Garrett to answer in his native tongue.

At the conference, the young couple found the Korean woman. They introduced Garrett to her. As she began to speak to the dark-haired boy, he suddenly grabbed onto his mother's legs. At the top of his lungs he screamed, " Momma, Momma, Momma!"

The parents realized this must have been where the longing to please them came from. Garrett was afraid they would send him back to Korea if he didn't act in a certain way.

Sometimes we need to get down on our knees to see life from the viewpoints of our grandchildren. Then we can treat them with the love and understanding they each need.

*Do not exasperate your children; instead, bring them up in the training and instruction of the Lord.*
EPHESIANS 6:4

> Grandparents can give grandchildren time and direction working parents may not be able to give.

As Jacqueline Kennedy stood forlornly at her husband's funeral, her thoughts were on her two children, Caroline and John. Just hours after the somber ceremony, still dressed in her black dress, Jackie hosted John's three-year-old birthday party at the White House.

From the time they were toddlers, through their teen years, and until they moved out, Jackie made her children her top priority. She was annoyed that the press pursued her children almost as much as they sought after her.

"I think it's hard enough to bring up children anyway. And everyone knows that the limelight is the worst thing for them. They either become conceited, or else they get hurt," Jackie once confided to a friend.

"Children need their mother's affection and guidance and long periods of time alone with her. That's what gives them security in an often confusing world."

The fact is, grandchildren grow up too. They will not always pull on their grandparents for a hug. When they get older, they won't beg you to read them a bedtime story. They will become too busy with their friends to want to bake cookies. They would rather be riding their scooters, roller blades, or bikes than going for a walk.

Enjoy the sticky fingers and endless questions for as long as they last. Cherish the interruptions and the middle-of-the-night requests. For when God sent grandchildren, He didn't intend for them to stay little forever.

*Honor one another above yourselves.*
ROMANS 12:10

A man went on a business trip to Houston the day after he returned from his second honeymoon celebrating his thirty-fifth wedding anniversary. His every thought was of his wife. He couldn't wait to see her again. On his way home, he stopped at a gift shop in the airport. He looked through numerous T-shirts, books, and magazines. He gazed at the dozens of gifts placed neatly on the counter. He finally settled on a bright white coffee mug that had the words *I love you* emblazoned in red on the outside.

> The world's best face-lift is a smile.

Knowing his wife's addiction to her morning coffee, he was confident the mug would be a treasured gift. So he had it specially gift-wrapped and held it closely to his heart during the flight home.

His wife met him at the airport. As he drove home, she happily chatted about their newest grandchild. Unable to keep the special gift a secret any longer, the man handed her the wrapped mug. He watched the road with a big smile on his face as she unwrapped it. He waited for a hearty "Thank you so much, honey. I love you too!" Instead, he heard peals of laughter. Slightly annoyed, he peered over at his wife as she laughed hysterically. He saw what was causing her to laugh. The mug said I love you on the front, but on the other side, the side he hadn't noticed, it continued—Grandpa!

That special gift was one that was chosen with the heart and also a gift that will be remembered forever.

*Rejoice with them that do rejoice.*
ROMANS 12:15 KJV

> ## To teach is to learn again.

Amanda worried about going to college. Would there be enough money? Would she like it? What if she failed? What would she major in? What if she didn't like her roommate? Her mother listened for many hours and then finally sent her over to Grandmother's house for some relief.

Lois, her Grandmother, listened for some time as Amanda poured out these worries. Then she gave Amanda a hug. "You know, dear, you probably had similar thoughts before high school. And God provided friends and all that you needed. I think you can trust Him with college."

Amanda laid her head on Lois' shoulder. "I guess so. It's just that the future is so scary for me. I don't know what is going to happen."

"I have things I worry about like that too, dear." She shared some of the things she was worried over.

"Wow, Grandma, I didn't know you had all this stuff to worry about!" said Amanda. "Well, maybe we can pray for each other."

That moment began a habit that changed Lois' life. In praying for Amanda, Lois found she could also begin trusting God for her own concerns, heavy concerns she had been, up to that time, carrying on her own. Amanda thrived in college and learned that prayer really could help her. And Lois found God loved her enough to help her with her everyday problems.

Ever notice that sometimes God gives us an opportunity to teach our grandchildren the very thing we need to learn? Think about the things you are teaching them now. Are your answers for you as well as them?

*Let the wise listen and add to their learning.*
PROVERBS 1:5

Bob Barker has hosted *The Price Is Right* for thirty years. The show debuted in 1956 and has aired over forty-five years. It has been rated the highest viewed daytime game show of all time. Its success has made Bob Barker somewhat of a cultural icon.

Bob's mix of charm and wit has helped earn the show fourteen Emmy Awards over the years. In the field of television, Bob Barker has certainly discovered his niche.

**Lots of play keeps your heart young.**

The contestants continue to whoop and holler as they try their hand at guessing the right price of the merchandise displayed. One thing that has changed over the years, however, is that college students have now become a large part of the audience.

"It has become a cult thing," says Barker.

In June 2001, Barker signed a contract for another five years with CBS. "I've done this all my life and have thoroughly enjoyed it," Barker explained. "I've been fortunate to get paid for something that I love to do. I have sympathy for people who dread going to their jobs. I feel blessed."[5]

While life is not all play and no work, many people have found that they enjoy their jobs so much that their jobs don't seem like work at all. We all have something in life that we are called to do. It may be in the form of work or play. Whatever we enjoy doing, we should work hard at it and make it a big part of our daily lives. For that is the key to true happiness.

*"I have come that they may have life, and have it to the full."*
JOHN 10:10

GLDB

> To be a grandparent, you
> have to be off your rocker—
> and on the move.

When Dan finally retired from his work, he took on more community and church activities. He became the chairperson of a large community project. He took the position as director over the church ushers. He became involved in a men's Bible study. And if that wasn't enough, Dan coordinated the neighborhood food drive. It seemed that the telephone never stopped ringing. The constant ringing was especially annoying on the two days a week that he and his wife kept the grandkids.

One afternoon, when his one-year-old granddaughter Haley took a nap, Dan decided it was time to spend some special time with his four-year-old grandson, John. He took John to the garage to show him his fishing lures and rods. About the time they got everything out and began enjoying each other's company, they heard the granddaughter crying over the baby monitor.

"Grandpa," John asked, "can't we just let the answering machine get it?"

At times we all need to turn on the answering machine in our lives and stop to listen to our hearts. We should take time out of our busy schedules for our children, our grandchildren, and for ourselves.

Life is nothing more than a vapor. It's here today and gone tomorrow. We shouldn't let outside activities take the place of inward emotions. We should be determined to enjoy every day to its fullest and on special days, when the grandkids are around, take John's advice and let the answering machine get it!

*Let us not become weary in doing good, for at the proper time we will reap a harvest if we do not give up.*

GALATIANS 6:9

The shy and withdrawn Anne Morrow married the adventurous Charles Lindbergh. She could have easily stood back and let her husband's success overshadow their relationship. Since he was the first person to cross the Atlantic by air, Charles was a national hero. Instead of becoming lost in the sea of admirers, however, Anne became one of America's most popular authors. Some of her best-selling books include, *Gift from the Sea,* and *Bring Me a Unicorn.*

> Grandparents have learned that encouragement is an important way to change lives.

Anne wrote of her husband, "The man I was to marry believed in me and what I could do. Consequently, I found I could do more than I realized." She attributed her great success to Charles.

Charles believed in Anne to an amazing degree. He saw beneath her shy exterior. He realized that deep down in her innermost being, a wealth of insight, profound wisdom, and an untapped well of ability could be found. Through his love, Anne discovered and developed her own skills. Charles encouraged her to do her own kind of flying.[6]

When a spouse believes in the other, great accomplishments can be made. With a little encouragement and love, even the most introverted person can become the person that God designed them to be. God made man and woman to help and encourage each other. When marriage partners lift up each other, they will not only fly, they will soar.

*Greet one another with a kiss of love.*
1 PETER 5:14

GLDB

## Grandparents use

## their words wisely.

A lady in her forties became acquainted with the computer. She loved the fact that she could e-mail people all over the world. When her friends started forwarding messages to her, she was really impressed and wanted to send them along to other people as well.

A young coworker was leaving the states to serve in a foreign country as a missionary. "Would you like for me to forward some of the messages that I receive?" she asked, when he gave her his e-mail address.

"That would be fine," he replied. "But please only send me things that I need to read. I won't have time to sift through the garbage to find the good stuff."

A few years later, the computer-literate lady became a grandmother, and she thought about the remark her friend had made years earlier. As a grandparent, we should only tell our grandchildren things they need to know.

They don't need to know that their parents forgot to send a Mother's Day card in 1996. They shouldn't hear about how the neighbors fight all the time. They don't need to be informed of the latest gossip that's being spread around the school.

Grandchildren need to hear words of encouragement, love, and support. They should be told happy stories. A grandchild shouldn't have to sift through the bad remarks to pick up on a few good stories. It's hard being a child in today's world. Shouldn't the words that he hears from his grandparents have a kind ring to them?

> *Do not let any unwholesome talk come out of your mouths.*
> EPHESIANS 4:29

Jay religiously believed in his nap time. To him, a nap was as important, if not more important, as mealtimes. As a matter of fact, he once made this comment: "I will miss a few meals, but I won't miss my afternoon naps." Even when the children or grandchildren were visiting, Jay stretched out, got comfortable, and took a snooze.

God gave us bodies that need to sleep periodically. He created us in His own image. And as an example, the Creator of the Universe rested on the seventh day. Doesn't that let us know that we need ample rest as well?

> A grandchild and an afternoon nap are the two greatest gifts a grandparent could ever receive.

Babies naturally sleep the majority of the time. Young children need to take a few minutes to slow down, rest their bodies, and also give their parents a break periodically.

Older folks need a little shut-eye too. By the time we get really old, we'll be sleeping a great deal of the time. So we may as well practice while we're still young enough to enjoy it.

If by reading this devotion you are finding yourself yawning, you have permission to place it on the bedside table and take a nap. It won't cost you anything. You'll feel more confident and refreshed when you wake up. And once you've rested you will have obtained the energy you need to finish reading the book.

Rest is an action deserved and a priceless gift. And wouldn't it be nice to have your grandchild cuddling closely to you to learn that lesson with you?

*Even during the plowing season
and harvest you must rest.*

Exodus 34:21

> Give your best to the
> world, and the best will
> be given back to you.

Jay Weinberg, his wife Martha, and fellow cancer survivor Herman Kotler founded an organization called Hospitality for Family and Friends Incorporated. This organization helps the family and friends of cancer patients, and sometimes the patients themselves, with lodging at unsold hotel rooms in New York.

One day, they received a call from a woman who had driven all the way from Michigan. She and her sons had come to take her husband to Memorial Sloan Kettering in New York City for treatment. She and the boys had nowhere to stay. Fortunately, a hospital social worker gave them the name and telephone number of this organization. They were able to find them a room free of charge.

Hotel accommodations are very expensive in New York City. Weinberg and Kotler are currently working with eight area hospitals and nineteen hotels that are willing to help.

A patient from Pennsylvania wrote these words of gratitude. "Your kind service provided me with peace of mind while going into surgery, knowing that my wife was safe nearby."

Every act of kindness is greatly appreciated. When a person is ill, alone, afraid, or apprehensive, the act is even more treasured. We all enjoy being servants and helping other people. When the need is the greatest, the servant is greatly blessed by God.

*"The more lowly your service*
*to others, the greater you are.*
*To be the greatest, be a servant."*
MATTHEW 23:11 TLB

Meredith and Jane, who were old friends, got together for lunch at their favorite restaurant. Meredith congratulated Jane on the recent marriages of both her son and daughter.

"How did you get it all done?" Meredith inquired. "Having two weddings in one month must have been very difficult."

Jane replied, "It was such a joy and an honor to help out with both my children's weddings. I was happy to do it."

"So tell me," Meredith gushed, "What kind of man did your daughter marry?"

> **Perspective comes with age. Gaining God's perspective comes with prayer.**

Oh," Jane sighed, "he is wonderful. He lets my daughter sleep in each morning. Sometimes she sleeps until ten or eleven in the morning. He tells her to go to the beauty parlor to get her nails and hair done as often as she likes. He even insists on taking her out to dinner every night."

"Wow!" exclaimed Meredith. "She is really blessed. Tell me about your new daughter-in-law."

"Well," Jane sniffed, "That's a *totally* different story. She sleeps in until ten or eleven every morning. She spends all of my son's money at the beauty salon getting her hair and nails done. And can you believe that she insists on eating every meal out?"

Life is about perspective. The way you look at things will affect your entire life and also the lives of those around you. Let's vow to see things from God's perspective. His viewpoint is always crystal clear.

*Let patience have her perfect work, that ye may be perfect and entire, wanting nothing.*
James 1:4 KJV

> # Today is the youngest
> # you will be for the
> # rest of your life.

Dance Outreach is an amazing program that assists more than 1000 disabled children. They are taught jazz, ballet, and tap, along with many other forms of creative dance. The founder is Zina Bethune. Zina was a former star ballet dancer with the New York City Ballet. Zina started her dance training at the tender age of six. At age sixteen, she learned that she had hip dysplasia. Doctors told her she would eventually loose the use of her legs. Zina chose to ignore their tidings of gloom. To this day, she continues to dance, regardless of the fact that she dances in pain.

In Dance Outreach, a child can be seen sitting in a wheelchair raising her arms above her head to form a blossoming flower. A blind child may wave a flowing scarf back and forth.

"Participation, not perfection, is emphasized in our classes," says Zina.

Adjustments to the dance are made as needed. A teenage boy with spina bifida pirouettes by spinning on his back.

"What we try to make clear," Zina explains, "is that their individual version of any dance step is valid. This is their own particular dance."

The Bible tells us that God can bring good out of any situation. At times, we don't feel like doing anything, much less dancing. But especially during the difficult times, we can choose to laugh when we feel like crying, smile instead of frowning, and dance when we feel like sitting out. Our children and grandchildren may be watching our every step.

*Make the most of every opportunity you have for doing good.*
EPHESIANS 5:16 TLB

Dottie loved creating beautiful things with her hands. She enjoyed making potpourri boxes decorated with ribbons and lace. She sat up nights to quilt. She found herself interested in calligraphy as well. She knitted homemade sweaters for the church craft sale, made her grandchildren matching outfits, and did needlepoint. This remarkable lady even made her own Christmas cards. You name the arts and crafts project, and Dottie loved to do it!

Her grandchildren loved to come for visits because they never knew what fun thing Grandma would be doing that week, and many times Grandpa was in the garage doing something interesting as a part of Grandma's creation. She was adventurous and unafraid to try anything. Grandpa was known to say with

> Isn't it amazing how much more fun a board game is when you're playing with a grandchild?

a smile that her adventurous spirit was just why he married her, and that he spent his life just trying to keep up.

And Dottie had simple crafts she set aside just for those visits so that everyone had something to make and take home. Her grandchildren learned to enjoy trying new things from their visits.

But as busy as she was, Dottie was never too busy to stop and spend time with her family and friends. Her hands might be busily stitching as she and Grandpa listened to a grandchild talk about school or a problem they struggled with, but she was up in a flash to bring in cookies and milk or to give a deeply needed hug. Dottie gave the works of her hands, but she also made time to give her heart.

It was no wonder her grandchildren were known to be just as creative and loving as Dottie.

*Wisdom brightens a man's face
and changes its hard appearance.*
ECCLESIASTES 8:1

> # The mind is like a parachute:
> ## it functions only when
> ### you open it.

Sometimes Jenna walked around the house with a frown and reacted irritably with everyone who spoke to her. Grandpa got impatient with her then. Her behavior made no sense. On one particular occasion, he began to wonder what was wrong with her. Why was she so quiet? And why did she refuse to talk? Puzzled, he decided to pray for her every day. God knew her secrets.

A few days later, the events of Jenna's life turned from bad to good. Jenna made the soccer team even though she had the flu. Her schoolwork was going well. She was suddenly a different gal! She came home all smiles.

Grandpa felt God prod him to talk to Jenna. He cornered her in the kitchen over a slice of apple pie. "Sometimes I don't understand your actions, Jenna. Why are you silent one day and then the next you become the happiest girl around?"

"I don't know, Grandpa," she said. "Sometimes I just don't feel like talking. I guess it's all a part of being a teenager."

"If you would talk to me, honey, maybe I could help you," he offered.

"I'll try," Jenna promised and gave her grandpa a big hug. They sat down to watch a soccer game on television. And Grandpa felt like God had led them both through an important turning point.

In life, human behavior can often seem mysterious and troubling. But God knows our hearts. Pray for those whose behavior mystifies you.

*If any of you lacks wisdom, he should ask God, who gives generously to all without finding fault, and it will be given to him.*

JAMES 1:5

Even though Neal was only six years old, he demonstrated a wonderful ability to draw and paint. His grandfather, Pa, was an observant man. He watched Neal draw sketches on plain paper and complimented his talent often.

Pa decided to help Neal expand on his talent and purchased all the supplies that an artist would need to paint a masterpiece. He gave these things to Neal, along with a great deal of encouragement. Neal used his artistic ability and painted a picture of a ship sailing the ocean blue, which continues to hang at his mother's home today.

When grandparents believe in their grandchildren, marvelous things can occur.

Since then, Neal has painted several portraits. He is one of the greatest wildlife artists ever. Over the years, he has painted and reproduced dozens of pictures, which hang on the walls of many homes and offices.

Grandchildren need to know that their grandparents believe in them. When an obvious talent surfaces, it is the parents' and grandparents' responsibility to help the child or grandchild make that talent grow.

That's exactly what Pa did for Neal. He saw both the ability and the potential in the child. He didn't stop there, however. He invested in the child's talent by purchasing the equipment he needed to get started.

When Neal used the materials that his grandfather provided, Pa was proud. He showed off the masterpieces to all his friends and beamed with delight, as each one complimented Neal's artistic ability.

When grandparents believe in their grandchildren, they will have the confidence to pursue their interests.

*May he give you the desire of your heart and make all your plans succeed.*

PSALM 20:4

169

# A child is always welcome at grandma's house.

A woman was visiting the home of her new friend. She felt somewhat inadequate when she realized that her friend lived a lifestyle of prosperity. As she entered the gated community and wound between elegant mansions, she felt anxious. Even her nice new car seemed a clunker passing the Mercedes Benzs and Jaguars. She spied her friend's house and, with a nervous draw of breath, pulled into the semi-circular driveway.

When her friend opened the front double doors, she spread her arms and openly exclaimed, "Welcome to Cinderella's Castle! Everything I have is yours!"

For the entire afternoon the lady of the house catered to her friend. She provided her with a fabulous luncheon and an intimate tea. The food was nice, but the thing that was remembered most was the laughter and the conversation that they shared together. They became best of friends that afternoon.

Hospitality and humility go hand-in-hand. The open door policy should be in existence regardless of the size of the house or whether it's decorated with gold or with wicker.

When our children or grandchildren come to our homes, it doesn't matter how nice the furniture is or whether the flooring is Italian marble or old linoleum. Charles Caleb Colton said, "A house may draw visitors, but it is the possessor alone that can detain them."

Make your family and friends feel right at home. But make especially sure your grand-children know that your house is a place where they are wanted. Welcome each of them with open arms.

*Share with God's people who are in need. Practice hospitality.*
ROMANS 12:13

New math these days confuses grandparents. But as they help their grandchildren with homework, they insist that, regardless of what you call it, one plus one equals two, and two plus two equals four.

Even grandparents need to review the arithmetic of time: we can't keep adding new activities to our agendas. If we already have five things to do and we add four more, we find ourselves with nine obligations. Our time is stretched to the limit, and we can't find time to do the things we need or want to do.

Grandchildren

spell love

T-I-M-E.

To successfully add more jobs to our already busy schedules, we must also learn how to subtract. When we only add and don't exercise our subtraction skills, somebody usually gets hurt. It is most often we or our spouses who get neglected. Heaven forbid, it could even be the grandchild who receives only the spare time we have left at the end of the month.

People who are living out their last days don't normally worry about how much work they didn't do over the years. They don't sit in a chair wishing they could go back to their busy activities or attend more community club meetings. Normally, when people are close to death, they have the desire to go back and spend more valuable time with their families.

Maybe this would be a good time to brush up on the arithmetic of time.

*Teach us to number our days aright,*
*that we may gain a heart of wisdom.*
PSALM 90:12

> You can't do anything about your ancestors, but you can greatly influence your descendants.

It wasn't until after Marjorie's death that her granddaughter Leah found a family tree. Marjorie had written it many years earlier in her own shaky handwriting. Leah rejoiced that at some point in Marjorie's life, she had known about her family's heritage and that she took the time to jot it down. What made it an even greater treasure was the notebook in which Marjorie had written all that she could remember of her parents, her grandparents, uncles, aunts, and cousins. The story of their faith and the trials they had come through successfully became a well of strength for Leah and her children.

Marjorie wasn't a movie star, a great politician, or even on the PTA Board. But she was Leah's grandmother, and for that Leah felt a strong heritage. She felt fortunate to have inherited the family tree that her grandmother had left. But even better than that, her grandmother left a journal of her life and the lessons God had taught her. Leah not only cherished it, but also shared it with her own grandchildren.

As a grandparent, don't sell your life story short. If you have someone who loves you, you have someone who wants to hear the story of your life. Tell them the stories of your life, the inspirations you have received over the years, and jot them down on paper. Share the lessons you've learned. Share your belief in God. And share the fact that you love your family and friends dearly.

Your story and the wisdom God has instilled over the years can influence not just your grandchildren, but their grandchildren as well.

*He decreed statutes . . .*
*which he commanded our forefathers*
*to teach their children,*
*so the next generation would know them.*
Psalm 78:5-6

Ten-year-old Katie was spending the week with her grandparents. "Grandma, may I take my dinner to the family room and watch TV," Katie asked.

"No," Grandpa interrupted.

"If you don't mind, we would like to all eat together," Grandma said. Grandma and Grandpa had decided earlier that during that visit they would discuss at least one character trait with Katie every day. So far that day, however, no character trait had come up.

*Think of something,* Grandma thought to herself.

> The best way to teach your grandchildren character is to have lots of it around the house, even when no one is around.

"Katie, do you remember when we were in the bathroom today at the rest stop? You missed the wastepaper basket when you were throwing away your paper towel. I was proud of you when you stopped and picked up the towel and put it in the basket."

"Yes," Katie answered. "I remember that."

"You could have saved yourself the trouble and left it there," Grandma explained, "and nobody would have ever known you did it."

Katie drew herself up to an adult posture and beamed.

"I think you're testing me. See if I pass the test. It's true that nobody was watching, but I know God sees what I do, even when nobody else is around."

"That's right," said Grandpa, smiling at his wife and then his granddaughter.

It's our character that controls the good things we do when nobody is watching. And it's our character that makes all the difference.

*As for me and my household,*
*we will serve the LORD.*
JOSHUA 24:15

> Grandchildren give us the opportunity
> to be the grandparents we wished
> we had when we were young.

In the book *Barefoot on Barbed Wire*, Christian singer/songwriter Cindy Morgan relates her grandmother's battles with fear. Unfortunately, Cindy's grandmother passed this character trait on to her kids and grandkids.

"Grandma was filled with fear. She never left the small community where she lived and, in fact, rarely left her house, except to attend church, shop for groceries, or pay a visit to the doctor," Morgan writes. "She never attended the weddings of her grandchildren, showed up for graduations or any other special occasions. She was absent at all the most important moments of my life.

"I'll never know what it would have been like to grow up with a special close relationship with my grandmother. Is it too late? Maybe not, but the bridge is long, and the water beneath is deep. And because of her fear, she can't even meet me halfway."[7]

Do you have painful memories of your grandparents? Or did you have ideal grandparents? Try journaling about some of your recollections, and come up with a list of desirable traits for grandparents. Whether we like it or not, many times we mimic the traits of our family members and loved ones. By writing them down, we can better evaluate what was good and what could have been better in our relationships.

Then ask God to give you the sensitivity, creativity, and tenacity to become the kind of grandparent for which every grandchild longs.

*Do not conform any longer to the*
*pattern of this world, but be transformed*
*by the renewing of your mind.*
ROMANS 12:2

I

If you're honest with yourself, how many times have you wondered if God is paying attention? Immediately following the events of September 11, 2001, many people flocked to churches, searching for answers.

On the evening of September 11, a mother was putting her children to bed. She asked them what they should pray about. Olivia thought they should pray for the people who had died that day. Six-year-old Clarke looked up with wide eyes and said seriously, "It must have been rush hour in Heaven today!"

> Do the things you can; then let God handle the things you can't.

This same family had recently suffered the loss of a very important man in their lives as a result of cancer. The children's grandfather was a vibrant, loving man who had died the year preceding the

September 11 terrorist attacks. There was no doubt that Olivia and Clarke, like thousands of other people, had spent many hours wondering why their loved ones had to die. But eventually, as we all do, the children had to put that question in the hands of God. Still, they have many questions. What is Heaven like? What's Grandpa doing now?

The Bible instructs us to come to Jesus as a child would: simply trusting. And God promises that when we trust, even in the midst of questions, peace beyond our understanding will fill us. God may not give us all the answers to every question, but His promises continue to remain true. He will never leave us, and He won't put more on us than we can handle.

*"Come to me, all you who are weary and burdened, and I will give you rest."*
MATTHEW 11:28

> A grandpa is a man who
> carries pictures in his wallet
> where money used to be.

In an article called "The Vacation Connection," Helena Koenig, grandmother of seven and founder of Grand Travel, says that leaving a legacy of memories can be more important than a grand financial estate. "Children don't know where money comes from," she says. "It has no personality. But they will remember experiences shared with grandparents."

"You have to plan it and make it happen," says Janet Colsher Teitsort, author of *Long-Distance Grandma*. "God commands us to pass on our faith and to be a godly influence in our grandchildren's lives. But if there's no connection, that's hard to do."[8]

Think of ways to create lifelong memories with your grandchildren. Create a notebook full of possibilities for future experiences.

Here are some ideas to get you started: go on a picnic; go to a local museum; invite grandchildren to go on vacation with you; create traditions on holidays; start a family newsletter or Web site; or create a loose-leaf journal in which you collect cards, letters, and e-mails from the grandkids.

An eighty-two-year-old grandmother of two, Mildred Williams wrote her memoirs and self-published them in a little volume called *Times Was*. Her family cherishes the book, because it gives them a glimpse of a time in their grandmother's life that they never knew.[9]

Memories of the good old days should be recorded and preserved. Once a memory is gone, it is lost forever, unless it's written down.

*A good name is to be chosen*
*rather than great riches,*
*Loving favor rather than silver and gold.*
PROVERBS 22:1 NKJV

His eyes moistened with unbidden tears as Nicole climbed into his lap and settled comfortably against his chest. Her hair, freshly shampooed and dried, smelled of lemons and touched his cheek, soft as down. With clear eyes, she looked expectantly up at his face, thrust the trusted and well-worn book of children's stories at him, and said, "Book me, Papaw, book me!"

"Papaw" James carefully adjusted his reading glasses, cleared his throat, and began the familiar story. She knew the words by heart and excitedly "read" along with him. Every now and then he missed a word, and she politely corrected him, saying, "No, Papaw, that's not what it says. Now let's do it again so that we get it right."

> Grandparents and grandchildren are good for each other.

She had no idea how her purity of heart thrilled his soul or how her simple trust in him moved him. James had had a far different childhood—one characterized by a demanding father. His father ordered him to work the fields from dawn to dusk beginning in his fifth year of life. His childhood memories sometimes continue to create anger and pain.

This first grandchild, though, has brought joy and light into his life in a way that supersedes his own childhood. He returns her love and faith with a gentleness and devotion that makes her world secure and safe. For Nicole, it lays a foundation for life. For James, it heals a past of pain.

Are their scars in your life? Let the love you give your grandchildren be part of the healing of your heart.

*Children's children are the crown of old men;*
*and the glory of children are their fathers.*
PROVERBS 17:6 KJV

185

> Ten years ago, I had five theories
> about being a grandfather.
> Now I have five grandchildren
> and no theories!

One size fits all doesn't work for Duane's grandchildren. James' visits are busy with all kinds of activities planned ahead of time to keep him busy. They go to the zoo and the park playground. But James, Duane has noticed, knows no strangers and can make friends with anyone and everyone. James can get a group of children who are strangers to each other involved in a game at the park and talking to each other on a first-name basis.

Amy and Angela come with their dolls and want to play quietly in the living room. While Duane barks good naturedly at James when he gets into things, he is careful not to startle Amy when she ventures timidly into the kitchen to ask Gramma for a cookie. Amy rewards his gentleness by making him one of her few confidantes, and each time they talk, he learns new things about the world as she sees it.

Erin and Cody love to build things with Grandpa in his garage, and Duane can do that because, unlike James, they are careful to listen to his instructions. Duane checks garage sales for tools to add to the toolboxes Erin and Cody have in Grandpa's workshop. They learned about the engine to the lawn mower last time and exhibited greasy hands to Gramma with great pride as they talked excitedly about each mechanical part and the tool best suited to take it apart.

Every child is different, Duane has found. And getting to know each new grandchild is a new adventure. He didn't have time to realize it with his own children, but Duane is beginning to understand God's pleasure in loving so many people.

Every one of your grandchildren is different. Celebrate their strengths and make allowances for their weakness.

*We are His workmanship,*
*created in Christ Jesus.*
Ephesians 2:10 nasb

Laverne remembers the day when, as a five-year-old child, she munched on animal crackers as she walked out of the grocery store with her grandmother, Ruth. It wasn't until they returned to their car that Ruth realized she hadn't paid for Laverne's snack. They raced back into the store to pay for the "stolen" item.

Thirty-eight years later, Laverne still remembers that lesson, as well as many more her grandparents taught her as she was growing up. She realized that her grandmother not only spoke of a life of integrity, she lived one as well.

> Sometimes the best conversation you can have with your grandchild requires no words.

Would you like your grandchild to grow up to be a man or woman of character? Children are constantly on the lookout for someone to model their lives after. What does your grandchild see when they look at you? Do they notice your honesty and kindness? Does your life tell them what they need to know about living right?

Laverne's grandparents lived an integrity-filled life. They taught her important truths by their actions and not simply by words. Now her goal as a parent is to pass the same legacy on to *her* children and future grandchildren. A grandparent has the opportunity to make a big difference in the life of a grandchild.

*You know how we lived among you for your sake.*
1 THESSALONIANS 1:5

## Relationships don't keep well in cold silence or intense arguments.

Wanda didn't have a good relationship with her daughter-in-law, Terry. The two of them had never gotten along. The situation became worse after Terry's first baby—Wanda's grand-baby—came along.

According to Wanda, the couple was much too private. They never wanted help with the baby. They often rejected her attempts to help them out financially, even though Wanda had plenty of money and wanted desperately to help out with the expenses of a new baby.

Wanda hated to see the young family struggle, when she felt she could make their lives easier. They were determined, however, to do things on their own and wouldn't accept her help.

After reading a Christian book about grand-parenting with grace, Wanda realized she had to let go of her expectations and hurts. If she was to have a good relationship with her son, daughter-in-law, and grandchild, she had to find peace within herself and allow the family to carry on in their own way.

Once Wanda forgave Terry for not being what she considered the perfect daughter-in-law, accepted the role that fit their particular family, and lightened up, she felt much better. Sometimes we follow God's way when we allow others to do things their own way and don't expect every situation to be what we feel is best.

*"In your anger do not sin": Do not let the sun go down while you are still angry.*
EPHESIANS 4:26

A woman sat on the floor of her grandmother's oversized walk-in closet. She watched intently as the elderly woman shuffled through disorganized boxes she had pulled off the shelves. She soon found the possession for which she had been searching.

"Here it is," she proudly announced to her granddaughter. "This is the ring your grandfather gave me when your mother was born. I want you to have it."

The granddaughter rose to her feet and gingerly accepted the ring. The fire from the stones was caught in the light and the woman gasped. "Oh, Grandmother, it's priceless."

"It cost my Herman a pretty penny," Grandmother replied.

> Sometimes things have value to your grandchildren simply because they once belonged to you.

As her granddaughter slipped the ring onto her finger, she said, "It's even more valuable to me because of what it represents."

The most important legacy we can leave those we love doesn't have a price tag hanging from it. The most priceless heirlooms are the lessons we teach our grandchildren about dignity, love, and honor through the examples of our lives. When we leave them with these valuable possessions, everything else they need will follow.

*He who pursues righteousness and love*
*finds life, prosperity and honor.*
PROVERBS 21:21

> A dad is a guy who gives his daughter
> away to a man who isn't good enough,
> so they can give him grandchildren
> who are better than anybody else's.

Ted wasn't too happy when his son, Andrew, announced his intentions to marry Susan. Ted felt Susan wasn't good enough for Andrew. She wasn't a college graduate. In addition, she had barely finished high school. Her current job, as a church receptionist, had no future. And Andrew often complained about his in-laws-to-be. Ted warned his son repeatedly about marrying Susan, but the couple went through with their wedding plans regardless.

Several years later, Susan and Andrew added two grandchildren to Ted's life. The kids, a boy and a girl just eighteen months apart, brought unspeakable joy to Ted's life. Little by little, his heart began to soften toward Susan. And after attending a men's retreat at his church, during a private prayer time, Ted confessed his lack of trust in God's sovereignty. During the retreat, which focused on giving thanks, God reminded Ted of Susan's exceptional qualities.

Her contentment in being a homemaker had enabled her to stay home with her children without remorse or regret. She was an excellent mother to them. After a lifetime of dealing with her overbearing parents, Susan had learned to set boundaries well for her own children. Ted's son Andrew had even learned how to handle his in-laws, after watching Susan in action. All these were blessings Ted had never been able to enjoy before.

Can you believe in God's sovereignty in your life and in the lives of your children? Take some time to sit in silence and ask God to speak to you about blessings you don't even know you have.

*There is surely a future hope for you,*
*and your hope will not be cut off.*
PROVERBS 23:18

It was just a broken seashell. As Janet held the shell closely to her heart, however, she realized that it had changed her outlook on life. Janet had taken a much-needed trip to the beach. She had felt that she had too much time on her hands. Her husband had recently passed away. She was tired, sad, and lonely. She wondered how she would go on with her life—alone.

The travel brochure promised sunny skies, soothing breezes, and seashells for the taking. On her first shell-hunting expedition, she was disappointed to find only broken shells. She couldn't find a perfect one anywhere. Still, she gathered up the broken pieces, placed them in her bucket, and walked back to her hotel room.

> The strongest and sweetest songs are yet to be sung.

Later, as Janet rinsed off the cracked shells, she felt ridges and other places worn smooth over time. There, upon closer look, where the protective outer shell had worn away, she found intricate, colorful twisting swirls. They were exquisite! And she would have never known about the unusual markings deep within the shells if she had found only unbroken shells.

At that moment, God spoke to her heart. She realized that the shells represented her own life. Like the shells, she was broken and cracked on the outside because of the pain she felt. But inside, she was beautifully and intricately woven. She had a purpose, even now. She felt a sense of peace and determination, knowing that God's plans for her were not finished yet.

*He put a new song in my mouth,*
*a hymn of praise to our God.*
PSALM 40:3

GLDB

> # Hearts become wings
> # when they are
> # opened by love.

Monica and her four-year-old daughter, Lisa, arrived just in time to help with dinner. Grandma greeted them at the front door, found a video to interest Lisa and then returned to the kitchen to finish preparing the evening meal. Monica was in the kitchen ready to help when her mother returned. The two ladies chatted as they cooked. Suddenly, they heard a loud thud, which came from the living room. Moving quickly, they found Lisa flat on her face, spread eagle on the floor.

Lisa began to cry when she saw her mother and her grandmother. "I can't fly," she wailed. The ladies held back their laughter as they realized Lisa had tried to fly like the character on the video.

"You are right," her grandmother told her, as she wrapped her arms around her. "You can't fly. God didn't give you wings. He gave you a brain to think, however. He also gave you enough talent that one day you will be able to soar higher than any bird."

Someone once asked the father of the renowned conductor Leonard Bernstein why he hadn't encouraged his son earlier in his life. He replied, "How was I supposed to know he would grow up to be Leonard Bernstein?"

Our little ones have the world at their fingertips and the ability to dream powerful dreams. Even children can be encouraged to be the best they can be. Encouragement lights a fire in their hungry souls. Positive support from parents and grandparents will also give them exactly what they need to fly as high as God would have them soar.

*Be imitators of God, as beloved children; and walk in love, just as Christ also loved you and gave Himself up for us.*
EPHESIANS 5:1-2 NASB

When Nana's sixteen-month-old granddaughter came for a visit, time flew by very quickly. It seemed that before she turned around, it was always time for the baby to return home. Before leaving after one particular visit, the little girl walked around the house and told all the pets goodbye.

"Bye, bye, Daisey," she said. "See you later, Sunshine and Blossom." She even went outside to wish a fond farewell to Benjamin Franklin and Snowball. "Bye," she shouted, as she waved and threw them all a kiss.

Nana and her precious angel went back inside to make sure they hadn't forgotten anything. They walked through the kitchen, where a picture of Jesus hung on the wall. "Bye, bye, Jesus," the little girl exclaimed. Nana smiled.

> Christian grandparents never say good-bye— they say "See you later!"

Saying goodbye is never easy, whether it is to a grandchild, a grandparent, or even to a family pet. The great thing, however, is that we never have to say goodbye to Jesus. He is faithful to travel with us and will always stand beside us. His presence can be felt in a million places at one time.

A grandmother can't be everywhere. Unfortunately, even though she would love to, she can't spend every waking hour with her grandchildren. A faithful grandmother can and will ask God to be ever-present with her grandchildren, however. And a trusting grandmother will have the assurance that God will stand guard over each of them until they meet again.

*Never will I leave you,*
*never will I forsake you.*
HEBREWS 13:5

> When you count your grandchildren, you are counting your blessings.

The five-year-old boy was spending a few weeks with his great-grandparents. Since they attended church on a regular basis, he joined them. He always wore a smile when he walked through the front door. His parents didn't take him to church, so the only time he heard about Jesus was when he visited his great-grandparents. They told him about how much Jesus loves him.

The little boy's grandfather passed away. For the sake of their great-grandson, his great-grandparents tried to be strong. "Your grandpa is in Heaven," his great-grandmother explained to him. "He's walking with Jesus."

A couple of Sunday's went by, and again the three of them attended the morning church service. The preacher talked about Heaven. "How is the best way to get to Heaven?" he asked.

The little boy spoke up and said, "You gotta die to get to Heaven!" While that may be true for the time being, one day Jesus is going to come again and take all of His children home. In the blink of an eye, lives will be changed forever. We should make sure that we are prepared to meet Jesus in the sky, and we should also make sure that our children and their children are prepared as well.

Heaven is a wonderful place and will be the eternal home for those of us who know Jesus in a personal way. Sometimes God leaves it up to grandparents and even great-grandparents to show His children the way home. Be sure you know the way, and be sure you show it too.

*"I am going away and
I am coming back to you."*
JOHN 14:28

Grunions do not lay their eggs in the water as other fish do. During the highest point of the tide, the tiny female silver fish flip up onto the beach in Southern California. There, the females wiggle their tails wildly to dig holes and lay their eggs, which are later fertilized by male grunions. The fertilized eggs remain dormant there for a month until the next tide once again reaches its highest point. When the salt water meets the eggs, they hatch spontaneously. Baby grunions are then swept out to sea.

> Grade school teaches children the facts; Gramma and Grandpa teach them the truth.

The mayor of Long Beach, California, shipped a grandmother a quart of sand taken from the high-tide mark where grunions lay their eggs. She placed a portion of the sand into a petrie dish, along with some salt water. She and her grandchildren watched in fascination while the tiny eggs, barely bigger than grains of sand, burst into life.

Children need both textbooks and life experiences to gain the knowledge they need in life. Textbooks teach basic facts, and life experiences teach them the mysteries of life that God created. Grandparents have the unique opportunity to teach both.

While a child could survive without knowing the science behind the grunion, isn't it nice that as grandparents we have the opportunity to teach them vital facts that they will use for eternity?

*I have chosen the way of truth;*
*I have set my heart on your laws.*
PSALM 119:30

The call of God on the life
of a grandparent is never to be
too busy for grandchildren.

## TO MY GROWN-UP SON

My hands were busy through the day
I didn't have much time to play
The little games you asked me to.
I didn't have much time for you.
I'd wash your clothes, I'd sew and cook,
But when you'd bring your picture book
And ask me please to share your fun,
I'd say: "A little later, son."
I'd tuck you in all safe at night
And hear your prayers, turn out the light,
Then tiptoe softly to the door . . .
I wish I'd stayed a minute more.
For life is short, the years rush past . . .
A little boy grows up so fast.
No longer is he at my side,

His precious secrets to confide.
The picture books are put away,
There are no longer games to play,
No good-night kiss, no prayers to hear . . .
That all belongs to yesteryear.
My hands, once busy, now are still.
The days are long and hard to fill.
I wish I could go back and do
The little things you asked me to.

—Author Unknown

Parents have many things they have to do and schedules they have to keep. Grandparents are usually different, however. Even though they may have things to do, they understand that nothing is as important as playing with a grandchild. Children don't stay young very long.

*Whatever your hand finds to do,*
*do it with all your might.*
ECCLESIASTES 9:10

Cheri's grandparents taught her that giving is better than receiving. Before Christmas one year, Cheri's grandfather designed a set of larger-than-life nativity figures for the town square. The entire family, including five-year-old Cheri, worked hard placing the figures in just the right spot for all to enjoy.

When Christmas morning arrived, Cheri received her most-wanted Christmas gift—a reindeer-shaped scooter with a "real" mane. Cheri was delighted. After the early morning Christmas festivities and the gift exchange, everyone in the household settled down to rest for a while. But soon the family awoke to the screams of Cheri's grandmother. She had discovered that Cheri was missing. The sun began to set as family

> Grandchildren are a great help in your old age—they help you get there faster!

members and neighbors searched diligently for the little girl.

Finally, a relieved neighbor called. "Come quickly, Mrs. Ivey. We found Cheri in the town square!" The family rushed to find a sleeping Cheri, curled up in the manger and cuddling baby Jesus. Her new reindeer scooter was standing beside the camels.

Her family gently woke her up, hugged her tightly, and asked her why she ran away. "I asked Santa to tell Jesus that if I got that reindeer scooter, I would give it to Him to play with. So I did. And I guess I just got a little tired."

Since Cheri's grandparents had been such wonderful models of sharing, giving became a natural part of Cheri's life. But Cheri passed along an even more important truth. Whenever you get a little tired, just snuggle up to Jesus, and He'll make it all better.

*Who is the one who overcomes the world, but he who believes that Jesus is the Son of God?*
1 JOHN 5:5 NASB

## Grandpa has his will,
## but Grandma has her way.

"I don't want to go, Grandpa," demanded Nathan. "I'll miss my favorite TV show." Nathan's grandfather Chet was disappointed in Nathan's apparent apathy toward spending time with him. He couldn't believe that Nathan would choose a television show over going on an overnight adventure in the mountains. Chet knew that the event would be one that Nathan would never forget.

Chet was ready to take all television privileges away from his grandson when his wife, Lois, spoke up. "Perhaps there is a more pleasant approach to this, Chet." She turned to Nathan and said, "Let's tape the program and watch it later, honey." Nathan finally agreed and got ready to go.

On the trip, Chet and Nathan sailed many miles by lashing two canoes together, using a tarp for a sail. They operated the locks between the two lakes and went down the spillway rapids. They built fires to cook their meals and told stories around the evening campfire.

On the evening they returned home, Chet and Nathan spent some happy hours reminiscing about the trip. Then Lois suggested they watch the television program that Nathan had missed. "That's okay, I don't need to see it," Nathan said.

Soon the boy yawned, stretched, and headed for bed. "I think we both learned some things as a result of our adventure," Chet shared with his wife.

It doesn't matter how young or old we are, there are always lessons that we can learn from each other.

*A wise man will hear, and will increase learning; and a man of understanding shall attain unto wise counsels.*

PROVERBS 1:5 KJV

Many people have the idea that lies are okay as long as they don't hurt anyone.

When Bill's grandchildren were young, he was surprised at how interested they were in the matter of truthfulness. "If you were to catch me telling you a lie," he asked them, "would you believe me the next time I told you something important? How long would it take before you could fully trust me again? Would you ever trust me again?" When he looked into their young eyes, Bill could see that the children understood his point regarding honesty.

> **If you tell the truth, you don't have to remember what you said.**

"Why don't we make a deal," he continued. "I promise before God and you that I will never intentionally tell you a lie. And I will put it in writing. It will be like a contract between us."

About a month rolled by, and Bill asked each of his grandchildren if they would be willing to sign an honesty contract with him. They were all eager to sign it. Over time, Bill saw that the contract really worked! He realized that his grandchildren were growing up to be men and women of integrity. He also noted that the lesson he taught them with the contract would be of great benefit to them throughout their entire lives.

Truthfulness is a lifelong comfort to its possessor. Honesty always has been and always will be the best policy. It's important that we impart this truth to our grandchildren while they are young.

*Truthful lips endure forever.*
PROVERBS 12:19

GLDB

> Make sure everything in
> your house is useful,
> beautiful, or delicious.

Once we have grown older, we have usually accumulated many trinkets and knick-knacks. Each and every figurine requires regular dusting. Clutter causes most people to feel overwhelmed and frustrated. Of course, each item carries a memory from the past, and some can't be parted with.

Another problem among the older generation is overstuffed closets and junk drawers. A grandmother needs to face the fact that she probably won't ever be able to fit into the size four she wore when she was in her twenties chasing after her three babies. A grandpa needs to realize that if it's almost impossible to open that junk drawer, he probably won't ever need anything stashed there.

A grandmother decided that she had too much. She started giving the things she didn't need to people who needed them. She gave her pastor's wife many of the books that had been given to her in years gone by. She took clothes to a local ministry and to a nursing home. She kept the trinkets that had special meaning and shared the others with the less fortunate.

She felt happy when she looked around her clutter-free house and realized that she had made her life much easier and, at the same time, had blessed many other people through her generosity.

All grandparents should take an inventory of their homes, give away the things they don't need, and rejoice in knowing that with less clutter to keep clean, they can enjoy spending more time with their grandkids.

*The Lord Jesus himself said:*
*"It is more blessed to give than to receive."*
ACTS 20:35

215

Patrick spent decades developing a career in law and missed his five children's childhoods as a result. When the grandchildren began to arrive, he surprised everyone by giving up his practice and opening a day care near his children. Now he is "Grandpa" to many other children besides his own.

"This is Jody," he says. "He wants to fly airplanes." The little boy smiles and runs off to swing in the playground. "This is Angela. She's going to be a mommy and a nurse." Angela smiles a grin with two front teeth missing and packs her dolls in a bag to go play with her friends. Patrick bends down to a shy, quiet girl who watches him and his guest. "This beauty is Amelia. She has high standards concerning whom she talks to." He

> Grandparents grow every time they kneel to help a child.

pulls out a stick of gum, which Amelia silently consents to receive. "Thank you," she whispers into Patrick's ear and runs off.

Patrick turns to his guest, once a fellow lawyer. "I left law after years of *pro bono* cases for divorce, crime, civil suits; almost all of them involved broken children. I was fortunate to have my wife who raised our kids right, while I was too busy to see them. But I feel it is time for me to give now. See that group over there? Those are my boy Tom's kids. I see them every day. I see Tom and his wife everyday too, when he picks them up."

You may have been busy during the years your children grew up, but you can change your priorities even now and put little people first on your daily agenda.

*"Blessed are the merciful,*
*for they will be shown mercy."*
MATTHEW 5:7

> A grandparent can add a great
> deal to a child's life by providing
> a gentle hug, an approving smile,
> or a simple compliment.

Jim was determined to spend some valuable time with his grandchildren. He looked for games to play with them and sought out inspirational stories to tell. All the while, he also looked for opportunities to compliment and encourage each of them.

He often said things like "God has a great plan for your life" and "You're an awesome kid." He'd ask them what they thought God wanted them to be when they grew up.

Many times Jim was impressed with his grandkids' responses to his questions. Sometimes he was even startled by the things they said to him. It surprised him how frequently the children wanted to discuss serious matters.

Jim bought a book filled with "conversation starters," at the local bookstore. He flipped through the pages, looking for things to discuss that would motivate his grandkids. Many times the children themselves brought up topics that were important to them. They always appreciated the serious discussions that they had with their grandfather.

Oftentimes, Jim took a devotional book to the table during mealtimes. He read appropriate topics once everyone had finished the meal.

Jim also took the time to pray with his grandchildren and to tell them how special they were before retiring for the night.

Jim knew that his efforts were not in vain, for the book of Isaiah—his favorite book of the Bible—says that the Word of God will not return void.

*As we have opportunity, let us do good to all people, especially to those who belong to the family of believers.*

GALATIANS 6:10

"I'm going to show you something today that you have never seen," said Earl Campbell, a Boys' Brigade leader. "Furthermore, nobody has ever seen this particular item before."

Earl proceeded to tell the story of Eli and Samuel. He finished by saying, "Please remember this truth: When God calls you, you may wonder if it is really God speaking. Or you may question if it is your imagination speaking to you. Don't worry about who is speaking. Simply answer as Samuel did with a sincere, 'Here am I.' Make yourself available to God. If it is truly God speaking, He will also be faithful to lead you in whatever direction He would have you to go."

At that point, Earl took from his pocket a peanut that was still in the shell. He broke it

> Children rarely respond to long speeches. But they are all ears if you let God make you His object lesson.

open and said, "No one has ever seen this peanut before." He popped the nut into his mouth and continued by saying, "Now no one will ever see that peanut again. Even though I enjoyed the peanut for a few seconds, now it is gone forever.

"If I had decided to plant the peanut, it would have grown and multiplied. Eventually it might have fed many people."

We never know when God calls us whether He is giving us something to nourish our own souls or whether He is giving us something with which to feed many other people. We should always be ready and willing to say, "Lord, here am I. Use me."

*The commandment is a lamp;*
*and the law is light; and reproofs*
*of instruction are the way of life.*
PROVERBS 6:23 KJV

GLDB

Tender moments and lasting memories are most often the result of sharing simple things.

"Oh, boy!" six year old Lucas shouted while talking on the telephone.

He asked if he could go to his grandparent's house the following Saturday. Lucas got the answer he wanted. "Can we go fishing too, Gramps?" Lucas followed.

Gramps hesitated for a few seconds. It wasn't that Gramps didn't like fishing with his grandson. He had already made plans for the day, however. Yard work, washing out the gutters, cleaning the garage, and washing the car were just a few of the chores on his agenda. But Gramps couldn't turn down his only grandson's request.

"Sure, Lucas," he answered. "We'll go fishing when you get here."

The day arrived, and being a man of his word, Gramps took Lucas to the lake. While they sat on the bank, holding on to their fishing poles, Lucas asked his grandfather many questions. Gramps answered them to the best of his ability. Lucas laughed and shared many things that only a grandpa could possibly understand. Between the two of them, they only caught one small fish. Lucas was quite excited about the catch, however.

At the end of the day, Gramps picked up his "to do" list. He thought about how he couldn't mark one single thing off of his list. At that moment, he overheard Lucas as he told his grandmother about the day.

"Oh, Grandma," Lucas exclaimed, "this was the bestest day! Me and Gramps fished, and we even caught something. Then we just talked, and I got to ask Grandpa lots of questions. It really was the *bestest* day *ever!*""

*I have learned, in whatsoever state*
*I am, therewith to be content.*
PHILIPPIANS 4:11 KJV

"Nana and Bumpa, are you coming to hear me play the recorder tonight at school?" Kailey excitedly asked her grandparents. Hardly giving a thought to their busy social calendar, they answered enthusiastically, "Yes! We'd love to come!"

Let's weigh some choices that grandparents of today sometimes have to make.

Tickets to the Philharmonic or front row seats at your grandchild's band concert?

Enjoying a candlelight steak dinner together or eating a quarter-pounder while watching your three-year-old grandson romp in the ball pit?

Keeping your morning ritual or volunteering to teach your six-year-old grandchild's Vacation Bible School class?

> I talked like a child, I thought like a child, and I played like a child. When I became a man, I put childish ways behind me. But now that I'm a grandparent, there's nothing that can beat listening and watching my grandchild talk like a child, think like a child, and play like a child!

Spending the morning at your ceramic class or taking your grandchild to the zoo?

Talking with your friend on the telephone or having a face-to-face discussion with an eight-year-old who wants to talk to you about the important things in his life?

Fulfilling your grandchild's requests may be inconvenient, but when weighed against the happy memories you will create for your grandchild and yourself, the answer is easy. Grandparents hold a special place in the hearts of their grandchildren, and they have a unique opportunity to make their grandchildren feel loved and cherished. With these things in mind, doesn't that quarter-pounder sound tempting?

*Never be lacking in zeal, but keep your spiritual fervor, serving the Lord.*
ROMANS 12:11

GLDB

> If you want to spend more
> time with your grandchild,
> find a hobby to share.

Gladys enjoyed being her granddaughter's Girl Scout leader. She laughed as she relayed to her friends what Amy had told her mother. "And next year, Grandmom and I will move into the older group. We will become *muffins!*" Of course the word she meant was *brownies,* not *muffins.* This childlike statement amused Amy's grandmother and all of her friends, but Amy's delight gave Gladys' heart an enduring glow.

Ben opened the mailbox one day, and to his surprise he found a package with his name on it. Tucked inside was a handmade, tri-cornered box sent to him from his grandfather. It's purpose was to store the Civil War hat that Ben had worn during the reenactment he attended with his grandfather. Although there was a thousand-mile difference between their homes, his grandfather knew Ben well enough to know what would be meaningful to him.

Laurie became ill during the Christmas holidays. She cried when she realized that she would miss all the Christmas parties that year. The party that upset her the most, however, was the one where her grandfather played the part of Santa. She was unable to attend the party, but the jolly ole man, also known as Grandpa, paid her a visit anyway. His thoughtfulness brightened her spirits.

Getting to know our grandchildren, their likes and dislikes, the treasures of their hearts, and the things that motivate them are of utmost importance. A grandparents' efforts will go a long way toward making the grandparent/grandchild relationship one that will be treasured by both.

*Whatever you do, work at it with all your heart, as working for the Lord, not for men.*
Colossians 3:23

In *The Grandmother Book,* Betty Southard and Jan Stoop write: "In dysfunctional families, children can often find that place of safety and unconditional love with Grandma. For them, Grandma can make a lifetime of difference . . . You can create a safe place for your grandchildren through your attitude, through your words, and through your actions.

"A grandparent can counteract negative attitudes, whether they are real or only exist in the child's mind. She can create a different atmosphere for the child. But remember, no parent wants his children to feel safer at Grandma's house than at his own home. The trick is to discover ways to counteract these negative attitudes without causing the child's parents to feel

> All children know that a grandparent is someone who greets you with a smile even when everyone else is frowning.

threatened. It's the balancing act again; it takes great courage and skill."[10]

In Luke 2:52, Luke wrote about how Jesus grew in wisdom and stature. Jesus also remained in favor with God and men. While God wants us to live for Him, He knows that we also should please our fellow human beings.

We must act in a spiritual way while at the same time living in this difficult world. Life is a great big balancing act. We want to be happy, but not at the expense of others. And we must remember that the kids we call our grandchildren are also our children's children. Ask God for creative ideas that will bless your children and your grandchildren at the same time. You'll be blessed too.

*He who covers over an
offense promotes love.*
PROVERBS 17:9

> It's important to treat your grandchildren as individuals with distinctly different personalities, talents, and abilities.

The dreariness of the day matched Will's mood as he walked into his once organized workroom. His grandson Daniel had come to visit. He had gotten into Will's toolbox and had left tools strewn everywhere. *Why can't he put things back where he found them?* Will wondered. *Didn't his parents teach him anything about organization?*

Susie's thoughts were on her granddaughter, Emma, who hadn't acted as if she enjoyed the party she had arranged for her and her friends. In frustration, Susie picked up the phone and called a friend. "It really was a fun party. But Emma didn't act very excited. Didn't her parents teach her anything about gratitude?"

Don sprang out of bed, exercised, and proceeded to get ready for work. During his drive to work, he thought of his grandson

Jake. *Even though Jake is a likeable kid,* Don thought, *he has no ambition. His grades are OK, and he has plenty of friends, but what will become of him? Didn't his parents teach him anything about ambition?*

Sometimes our grandchildren don't act in a way that we think they should. However, some conflicts may simply be the result of personality differences.

Daniel may be messy, but he has social skills that will take him far.

Emma doesn't show her feelings, but she can organize anything.

Jake appears lazy, but he is a wonderful mediator and a friend to many.

As grandparents we can appreciate our grandchildren for who they are and look for their good points. If we major on the positive things we observe in them, we can effect a transformation in their lives that may surprise us.

*Now the body is not made up of one part but of many . . . God has arranged the parts in the body, every one of them, just as he wanted them to be.*

1 CORINTHIANS 12:14,18

Have you ever noticed that the older you get, the more insignificant trivial things become? Can you laugh at yourself now a little more than you used to?

If not, here are some ways to lighten up:

Make fun of your forgetfulness by calling it a "senior moment."

Call your fiber drink a "milkshake for Grandmas."

Describe in great detail what the inside of your eyelids look like, after yet another nap.

For Christmas, request a kid's educational computer game, so you can increase your eye/hand coordination and other computer skills.

When grandchildren ask where all your hair went, point to your ears and nose.

> Grandparents are people who can afford to make jokes at their own expense.

Count your blessings when you have so many people in your family that you get their names mixed up. Throw in your pet's names once in a while.

Tell your grandchildren that you sit a lot because it creates a lap for them to sit in.

As we grow older, we might start doing some odd things. But our quirks are endearing traits to those who love us—especially if we share a good laugh together.

*He will yet fill your mouth with laughter and your lips with shouts of joy.*
JOB 8:21

> There are many ways to measure success. For a grandchild, it comes down to how their grandparents lovingly focus on their good points.

When Charles William Eliot was a young Bostonian in the 1800s, an unattractive birthmark on his face concerned him. He made several appointments with surgeons in hopes of having it removed. He was told time after time, however, there was nothing that could be done about it. Distraught and discouraged, he sought the comfort of his mother.

"My son, it may not be possible for you to get rid of that hardship," she encouraged, but it is possible for you, with God's help of course, to grow a mind and a soul so big that people will forget to look at your face."

Eliot chose to follow his mother's advice. In 1869 he became the twenty-second president of Harvard University. He held this position for forty years. Under his presidency, the small college grew into a mighty university. Eliot took on the responsibility of forming new schools and aided in the development of the Radcliffe Institute for Advanced Study.

No doubt, Eliot's extensive accomplishments were due to a mind and soul so big that Eliot eventually forgot about the birthmark that had once haunted him. The United States showed great honor to this man when his face, marred by a birthmark, appeared on a postage stamp.

Although all grandparents think of their grandchildren as perfect individuals, sometimes our grandchildren don't see themselves in quite the same light. It is our responsibility to teach our grandchildren to look beyond the obvious and see the incredible persons they really are.

*As water reflects a face,*
*so a man's heart reflects the man.*
PROVERBS 27:19

Jill received the letter, written by her grandmother, in the mail on her sixteenth birthday. "Dearest Jill," the note read, "I can't believe how you have grown! And now you are a young woman of sixteen. As you know, I write each of my grandchildren a letter on their sixteenth birthday, telling them what they mean to me. You, my dear, are a true blessing and a joy. Your bright smile never fails to encourage me. Your warmth and affection lift my spirits each time you come to visit. You are a great student and an honest, hard worker. You are also a responsible teenager.

> One of the most important parts of a grandparent's job is to nurture self-esteem.

"I know your parents were thrilled when you received another award at the school's end-of-the-year assembly. But more than what you do, I want you to know that I love and admire you because of who you are. You are a sweet, gentle, and Godly Christian.

"Know that I am praying for you as you make the difficult decision about where you will attend college. Also remember that your mom, dad, and I are praying diligently for you to find the right man with whom to share your life. He is going to have to be someone very special to be worthy of our Jill! With love, Nana"

Jill kept the letter in a safe place and pulled it out whenever she felt discouraged or needed a little lift. A well-written letter is a way to express meaningful sentiments that will continue to encourage, long after you are gone.

*"Are not five sparrows sold for two pennies?*
*Yet not one of them is forgotten by God.*
*Indeed, the very hairs of your head are*
*all numbered. Don't be afraid; you*
*are worth more than many sparrows."*
LUKE 12:6-7

> ## Stay alert! Even infants have been known to outsmart their grandparents.

Ned and Frieda came to help celebrate their granddaughter Jaycee's second birthday. Jaycee's mom left Jaycee in the care of her grandmother while she went shopping for a few last-minute items.

Jaycee played contentedly with her dolls on the floor while Frieda was busy putting on her makeup in a nearby chair. The telephone rang. Frieda ran to answer it, leaving her makeup and tweezers on the chair. Within seconds, Frieda heard a loud *pop!* The lights flickered. Frieda dropped the telephone and ran to find Jaycee.

Jaycee had picked up her grandmother's tweezers and stuck them into a nearby outlet. Frieda rushed to Jaycee, picked her up, and held her tightly in her arms. Jaycee began to cry. Frieda cried as well. She looked down at the tweezers in the outlet. Fortunately, the electrical surge protector shut down at the first inkling of trouble, saving Jaycee's life.

"Oh, Lord, thank You!" cried Frieda. The gratitude that Frieda felt that day was overwhelming.

Each day that we live, we should be grateful for the times that God has kept us safe and out of harm's way. We'll never know how many times our grandchildren have been in dangerous situations, but the Lord was standing nearby protecting them. Expressing thanks for God's daily protection is crucial to finding peace in a dangerous and trying world.

*The LORD protects the simplehearted.*
PSALM 116:6

A father of two said, "I try to affirm my kids every day. The outside world is so negative, and I want them to truly believe in themselves and know that I love them. I don't think we can tell our kids enough how great we think they are." The same goes for grandparents.

Following are phrases from *Mom's Devotional Bible* that the grandkids would love to hear you say to them:

Wow! Way to go! Super! You're special! Outstanding! Excellent! Great! Good! Neat. Well done. Remarkable. I knew you could do it! I'm proud of you. Fantastic! Nice work. Looking good. You're on top of it. Beautiful. Now you're flying! You're catching on. Now you've got it. You're incredible. Bravo.

> Grandparents make great cheerleaders.

You make a good friend. You make me laugh. You make me happy. I love being with you. You're terrific. You mean the world to me. You're a joy. You're A-OK. Hurrah for you. You're on target. You're on your way! How nice. How smart. Good job. That's incredible. Dynamite! You're unique. You're beautiful. You're a winner. I like you. Spectacular! Fantastic job. Hip, hip, hooray! What an imagination. You're so responsible. You're growing up. You tried hard. You did your best. I respect you. I admire you. You're my hero. You made my day![11]

The ring of these words would make any child, or adult as far as that goes, sing. Tell someone how great he or she is today. Go ahead—make their day!

*We loved you dearly—so dearly that*
*we gave you not only God's message,*
*but our own lives too.*

1 THESSALONIANS 2:8 TLB

Every good grandparent knows
that giving children everything
they want is a good way
to make them miserable.

Renée Wheeler, a grandmother and leader of Mothers of Preschoolers International, listened to her daughter express the concerns she had about her son. "He expects to have everything he wants," she confided in her mother.

In a MOPS newsletter, Renée asked these questions: "How do we teach our children to be givers, not takers? How do we instill in them an attitude of gratitude?" She also shared the discussion she had with her mother.

As the two ladies put their heads together, they concluded that as parents and grandparents, they were to model the proper way to show gratitude. "Our children watch us all the time," one of the ladies noted. "What we show our children about gratitude will influence how grateful they will become later in life."

Secondly, Renée and her daughter decided that they should not give in to every demand the child makes. They concluded that there is nothing wrong with saying no or having a child earn a special treat or privilege. It takes a determination not to give in to all of their requests, but it is worth it.

Many times, God speaks to His children regarding this issue too. He gives us the things we need, but at times, we beg for things we don't need. He doesn't give in to us because He knows the big picture and is aware of the things that are good for us. When God answers our prayers—even when His answer is no—we can continue to approach Him with a thankful heart because He has thought about our lives very carefully and gives us what is best.

*The rod and reproof give wisdom: but a child left to himself bringeth . . . shame.*
PROVERBS 29:15 KJV

Words have the potential to make a person feel loved, respected, and honored. They also have the potential to make a person feel belittled, uncomfortable, and sad. Such words can cause a person to cry, withdraw, or even give up on life.

Just because a child is little doesn't mean that words can't cut, bruise, and damage their hearts. Children are the world's worst at saying words that hurt to other children who are supposed to be their friends. Unfortunately, parents and grandparents can say words that hurt as well.

When another child says something hurtful, most of the time it is forgotten over time, but when a parent or grandparent makes a careless remark, it will probably never be forgotten. That child will carry that remark for as long as they live.

> When you feel like you just have to say something—that may be the most important time to hold your tongue.

Too often adults say things that they don't mean. Words can slip out in bursts of anger or frustration. Kids believe what they hear, however. They don't understand the difference. So what's a parent or grandparent to do when they slip up and speak hurtful remarks?

A hug and an apology will go a long way. Trying to do better the next time can make all the difference.

In *Words that Hurt, Words that Heal,* Carole Mayhall wrote. "I want to be a woman of knowledge and understanding. But do you know some of the characteristics of such a person? A man of knowledge uses words with restraint, and a man of understanding is even-tempered. Even a fool is thought wise if he keeps silent, and discerning if he holds his tongue."[12]

*Everyone should be quick to listen,*
*slow to speak and slow to become angry.*
JAMES 1:19

> # Becoming a grandparent
> # is much easier than
> # being a grandparent.

You need a license to drive a car, a boat, or a motorcycle. To go fishing, you need a fishing license, and to hunt you must purchase a hunting license. A marriage license is required before you say, "I do." You must have a license to practice medicine, work on teeth, or represent a person in a court of law. A teacher must be licensed to teach, and a nail technician has to be licensed to do nails.

You don't need a license to become a parent or a grandparent, however. There is something odd about this situation. Being a parent or a grandparent is by far the most important and challenging profession you will ever have. In eternity you will answer to God for how you treated the children in your life. Were you kind or abusive? Did you show patience or expect the child to be patient with you? How did you measure up as a parent or grandparent?

If we are to become successful in raising children, we need to obtain the proper skills. There are many ways of doing this. Classes on raising children are offered free of charge in almost every city in every state. Numerous books and Web sites offer helpful advice to the parent or grandparent who has questions. Consulting with a counselor or teacher can help a person to discover the right way to discipline a child. But the most important source of information can be found by searching the Scriptures. The Bible is an instruction manual for living. There you can find everything you need to know.

*Listen to advice and accept instruction,*
*and in the end you will be wise.*
PROVERBS 19:20

"Wow, Grandma! Look how pretty the frost is on the grass!" a small girl shouted on a cold winter morning.

"How can God make every one of these snowflakes different?" a little boy asked.

"Just how big *are* those stars?" a grandchild asked, after gazing through his grandfather's telescope.

God's creation is so magnificent that we will never understand every-thing about it. Like our grandchildren, we also ask questions regarding the wonders of life.

> The best grandparents are those who have not lost their sense of childlike wonder.

"Will it ever rain, Lord?" a farmer may ask. "The crops are getting mighty thirsty."

"Where will our next meal come from, Lord? The cupboards are bare, and there's no money in the bank," the single mother may say.

Many times in life, we think we can't make it another day. We worry about our children and grandchildren and if they will be OK after we are gone. But the wonder of it all is that God always provides for our needs. Many times, we look back and wonder how it has happened. When we think back, we realize that God provided the things we needed even better than we had expected.

While children ask questions, they usually ask because they are interested in learning more. When adults ask God questions, they are normally either worried about something or seeking something they don't have. Jesus has asked us to come to Him as a child, and He has promised to welcome us with open arms. As a grandparent, do you have any questions for God today?

*"I tell you the truth, anyone who will not receive the kingdom of God like a little child will never enter it."*

MARK 10:15

> Our grandchildren give us a second chance to do the things we wish we had done with our own children.

Unfortunately, Nate grew up in an angry household. His mother was angry with his father for coming home drunk most evenings. His father drank because he felt that he had no choice but to struggle with a dead-end job. While the anger in the household grew, so did the resentment between the family members.

As a result of his upbringing, Nate never learned proper parenting skills. He followed in his father's footsteps and became an angry father. Fortunately, Nate stayed away from alcohol, which eliminated one problem. But instead, Nate became a workaholic. He spent very little time with his children.

When his children became teenagers, Nate attended a men's Bible class with a friend. For the first time in his life, Nate began searching for a sense of peace. As a result, Nate gave God top priority in his heart. He apologized to his family for his past behavior. It took time, but with God's help, his family was able to fully forgive him for his actions.

Nate was thrilled when both his son and daughter presented him with grandchildren within a few months of each other. Nate found the second chance for which he had desperately prayed. He offered to keep the grandkids while they were young. He sent them encouraging cards, letters, and e-mails when they were old enough to read. When they approached the teenage years, Nate showered them with his time, attention, and affection. In turn, Nate's grandchildren gave him unconditional love, something that he never received as a child.

Never think it is too late to change. There is still time to enjoy your children and grandchildren.

*We know that all things work together*
*for good to them that love God, to them*
*who are the called according to his purpose.*
ROMANS 8:28 KJV

Jennie's parents died in an accident when she was ten. Her grandparents took care of her after the accident. By the time Jennie became a teenager, she resented their household rules. On her fifteenth birthday, Jennie packed her belongings and walked to the nearest bus station. She had an online friend who lived in California. This so-called friend, a man who habitually preyed on troubled girls, promised to help her get into modeling school.

Two months later, Jennie hit rock bottom. The man was a child pornographer. She barely escaped his clutches. By that time, she was broke and hungry. She slept restlessly under park benches, if she slept at all.

Suddenly, Jennie realized what a wonderful home she had left. She knew that her

> Grandchildren need your time—especially when they don't deserve it.

grandparents loved her dearly. And she realized how much she loved them too. Jennie sold her mother's wedding ring, the only thing of value she had left, and bought a ticket home.

In the middle of a sunny afternoon, she trudged down the street toward her grandparents' house. She wondered what kind of questions they would ask her. She also worried about how she would answer their questions.

When she glanced up, she saw her grandma and grandpa running toward her with their arms open wide. There were no questions asked. The only words exchanged between the reunited family members were words of love, hope, and forgiveness. Jennie was home. Everyone was happy.

*Above all, love each other deeply, because love covers over a multitude of sins.*

1 PETER 4:8

GLDB

> Measure wealth not by
> the things you have, but by the
> things you have for which you
> would not take money.

Tom grew up in a poor home. His family never dined out. As far as he could remember, he had never traveled outside of Pennsylvania, except once to visit a gravely ill uncle. Since Tom never heard his parents fret about the lack of money, he didn't realize that he was poor. His parents worked hard for a living. As a result, Tom knew that he had to work hard, as well.

Once he completed high school, Tom joined the United States Navy. He began traveling all over the world. He saw places he had never seen before. He received a regular paycheck. He felt fortunate to have been brought up to appreciate the simple things in life.

One day, Tom received a handwritten note of encouragement that shed light on his parents' good example and training. It read something like this, "You cannot tell of a man's wealth by turning to his wallet. Rather, it is the heart that reveals whether a man is rich or poor."

As far as Tom was concerned, he was the richest young man in town. His parents loved him, while so many of his friends felt unloved by their parents. He was taught to appreciate things, while others begged for things they couldn't afford.

Regardless of how rich or poor we are monitarily, God wants us to know that He loves us. He also wants us to appreciate all of the things, whether big or small, that He has given to us.

*"What good will it be for a man if he gains the whole world, yet forfeits his soul?"*
MATTHEW 16:26

Jim stumbled onto a game to play with his grandchildren, which, surprisingly, became a great hit.

"Amy?" he called from the front seat of the car. He got no answer.

"Kim," he continued, "is Amy back there?"

"No," Kim laughed, "Amy jumped out at the last stop light!" He heard Amy snicker.

"Oh dear!" Jim tried to sound alarmed. "Will you help me look for her?"

Kim didn't respond.

"Kim?" Jim said again. He heard soft laughter, but not a single word came from the backseat. Jim began talking to himself. "What on earth will I tell their parents when I get home without them?" From the backseat came more muffled snickers.

> Play with your grandchildren. They'll teach you how to be young again.

When they arrived home, Jim deliberately took his time getting out of the car. The kids jumped out of the backseat and ran and sat down on the front porch. There they coolly awaited Jim's arrival.

"What took you so long, Grandpa?" they asked and then burst into toothless giggles.

The game worked so well as entertainment on car trips that Jim tried it out on his other grandchildren, Mick and Jennifer. Instead of disappearing, they turned into animals in the backseat, complete with sound effects. Jim complained bitterly, trying not to laugh.

Many relationships have been made better when people stopped being so serious and began to play games together. Playing *I spy,* or other travel games like *Name That Tune* when the radio is playing can create fun memories that will last forever.

*May the LORD bless you from Zion*
*all the days of your life; may you*
*see the prosperity of Jerusalem, and*
*may you live to see your children's children.*
PSALM 128:5-6

> There are two priceless gifts
> we can give our grandchildren:
> the first is roots; the other is wings.

Jenna's teacher read a lovely story to her class about a bird that had broken its wing. "Why can't the bird fly anymore, Grandpa?" Jenna asked. "Jimmy broke his leg last year. He went to the doctor, and now he can walk again. He is just as good as new."

"Well," said her wise grandfather, "when boys and girls break bones, they heal quickly. Doctors can attach splints, insert pins, put on casts, or even perform operations if necessary. After one or more of these things is done, a person's bones can heal properly."

"Why can't we take care of the birds in the same way?" asked Jenna.

"We can do some things when we find them. Unfortunately, many times the wing heals crookedly, and the bird can't fly high anymore."

Like a doctor with his patients, one of the special gifts a grandparent can offer a grandchild is a grandparent's ability to see quickly when events have hurt them. They can then quickly step in to offer encouragement and healing. Often grandparents can only pray, but many times their prayers are just what the child needs.

Do you see some problems that could keep your grandchild from flying high? Step in to help and express love and encouragement if you can. But pray first, and you can be confident that God will orchestrate a thousand small events in their lives to keep them whole.

*If the root is holy,
so are the branches.*

ROMANS 11:16

"Lindsey, I'm looking forward to the time where you're old enough to act young again!" said her mother, Mary. Thirteen-year-old Lindsey felt self-conscious about everything. She worried about the way she looked, the way she acted, and even about her relationships with other people.

As grandparents, we can look back on those times in our own lives and remember how hard life was as a teenager. As we grew older and more self-assured, we gradually drew our values from God, not people. God knew what he was doing when He gave us only a few teenage years to live through.

Now many of us have come full circle. We live like carefree children again. But to make

> **It takes a long time to become young.**

things even better, we have lived life and have gained a great deal of wisdom over the years. We have learned that it doesn't matter how we look, as long as we're clean and neat. We draw our strength from God's love and pass that special accepting love on to our family and friends.

Sherry, a grandparent of five, once made this remark. "I want to enjoy the season that I am in because I know each season is wonderful and brings with it new learning experiences. I don't want to be young again. I want to stay youthful. Youth is not an age, but a frame of mind. It's also a choice that we make for ourselves."

*Those who hope in the LORD*
*will renew their strength.*
*They will soar on wings like eagles;*
*they will run and not grow weary,*
*they will walk and not be faint.*
ISAIAH 40:31

> The pleasure of any activity is
> doubled when shared
> with a grandchild.

In *Basket of Blessings,* Karen O'Connor wrote these words: "'Over here, Magah,' my grand-daughter shouted. 'Look at all these pretty ones.' I moved down the beach to where Johannah was sitting. Her cup was already half-full of beautiful seashells. She spread them out for me to see. 'Can I keep them?' she asked.

"'Of course,' I replied. 'Let's clean them up. Then you'll have some beautiful souvenirs to remind you of our day together.' We washed each one, noticing how the pink, yellow, and pearl-colored flecks danced in the sunlight as we rinsed away the grit. 'God, your creation is so awesome. You are so good to me,' I said as my eyes teared. I couldn't imagine anything more wonderful than that moment with Johannah on the beach."[13]

What kinds of memories do you have with your grandchildren? Do you cherish the simple moments? Have you ever considered the art of being fully aware of every moment that you spend with your grandchild?

Seeing joy in a grandchild's eyes is better than witnessing the most beautiful sunset. Seeing hope when things in life are not going so well is better than any gift that could be purchased. A few sweet words like "I love you, Grandma" are music to the ears and bring joy to our hearts. But none of these things can be obtained if we don't spend the time seeing, listening, or feeling. Life is truly a basket of blessings. Won't you give yourself time to feel blessed today?

*My people will receive a double portion,*
*and instead of disgrace*
*they will rejoice in their inheritance;*
*and so they will inherit a double portion in*
*their land, and everlasting joy will be theirs.*
ISAIAH 61:7

Most people like a clean and organized home. There are some messes we love, however, and may even want to preserve. After our grandchildren leave, we may notice a few scars where they had been playing.

The twins chewed on the stereo cabinet as they enjoyed the music playing. Crayon marks cover the high chair tray. Dark stains on the carpet represent spilled juice. Although you may not be thrilled with these additions to your decor, you proabably smile as you reflect on how precious your grandchildren are to you.

A grandchild may leave your home— but never your heart!

The walls are marred with chocolate hands, and growth charts can be found written on the wall in the utility room. We hesitate to paint over or fix these things. They serve as happy reminders of days gone by and help to keep us feeling young and in love with our grandchildren.

What kind of marks will we, as grandparents, leave behind in our grandchildren's lives? Will they remember us as the ones who constantly said no, or will they remember us for our smiles, love, and support? When they think of God and the love He has given to the world, will they remember that we played a role in explaining the spiritual insights they received?

A grandchild who remembers his or her grandparent as a fun member of the family and not as a grandparent who was constantly running around with a mop and broom in hand will have happier memories later in life as a teenager and adult.

*How can we thank God enough for you in return for all the joy we have in the presence of our God because of you? Night and day we pray most earnestly that we may see you again.*

1 THESSALONIANS 3:9-10

> ## There's more to being a grandparent than merely having grandchildren.

Christian author Eva Marie Everson claims her family tree is actually a forest. In her book *One True Vow,* she writes, "The day we married, my [Dennis] presented me with two very special gifts: my stepchildren, Christopher and Ashley." In 1981, the Eversons welcomed Jessica, and eighteen years later, they added a fourth child—Sarah, twenty-two—in what the family calls "an adoption of the heart."

Their son Chris married Kathleen, who had a son, Jordan. They later welcomed Savannah into the fold. After adding Sarah's daughter, Jordynn, the Dennis Eversons have three grandchildren.

"Our family tree is made up of many branches," Eva Marie says. "But they have the same root."

Weeks after Jessica was born, one of Eva Marie's stepchildren questioned whether the baby was a "real" sister, resulting in a new family motto: "What's not bound in blood is bound in love. In this family there are no halfs or steps. There is only family."[14]

Being family goes beyond chromosomes. In modern families, where trees become forests, it is important for grandparents to treat all their grandchildren equally—without prejudice. A good grandparent realizes that all children are the most precious commodity life offers. Where they came from is not important. They all need an equal amount of love to be able to be the best they can be. Accept all your grandchildren. Love each of them with your whole heart.

*Be kind to one another, tenderhearted,*
*forgiving one another, as*
*God in Christ forgave you.*
EPHESIANS 4:32 RSV

J

Just as there are many different kinds of grandparents, there are also many different ways to grandparent. In *A Letter Is a Gift Forever* by Florence Littauer, contributor and grandma Pat Damon shares some original ideas: "With the birth of each grandchild, I wrote a simple note to welcome them. To make the note even more personal, I traced around my husband's hand, then mine inside of it. We instructed the parents that as the child grew older and knew who we were, they were to show the child the hands and place his little hand in ours.

"Because I didn't want to be called 'Granny' or 'Grandma,' I came up with fun names for my husband and me. I'd be Lolli, and he'd be

> A happy childhood is one of the best gifts grandparents can give their grandchildren.

Pop. When we visit, they call out 'Lolli and Pop are here!'"[15]

Grandparents have the opportunity to make life fun for the little ones. The have the time and creative ability to make a child laugh. Telling jokes, teaching them happy songs and nursery rhymes can make each day delightful.

Even telling them stories from the good old days can bring amazement to their eyes. And they love hearing stories about their mommy and daddy when they were young. Who could possibly remember those stories of old better than Grandma or Grandpa?

When the grandkids come, pull out the old picture books. Look back, laugh, and giggle the day away. You'll earn lots of hugs and kisses in the process.

*May the righteous be glad*
*and rejoice before God;*
*may they be happy and joyful.*
PSALM 68:3

> Grandchildren are spoiled
> because parents can't
> spank the grandparents.

Nana took her sixteen-month-old grand-daughter, Hannah, shopping. "Here you go, honey," Nana said as she handed her a cute stuffed animal. Hannah took it in her arms, hugged it, and handed it back to her grand-mother. "Put it back," she said.

Nana assumed that the baby didn't like that particular toy. She wanted to buy her something, so she pushed the shopping cart to the toy department. Hannah looked around and smiled. Nana handed her an activity center. Hannah punched a few buttons and handed it back to her Nana. "Put it back," she whispered. They went home empty-handed.

A couple of weeks later, Nana and Pa joined Hannah's family at an amusement park.

Nana spied a precious stuffed animal on a gift stand. She picked it up, handed it to Hannah, and asked, "Do you like this Hannah?" Hannah smiled, hugged it, and handed it back, saying, "Put it back." Hannah's parents then explained that they had been teaching their daughter that she couldn't have everything she wanted.

As grandparents, we can't have everything we want either. We have to give up some things to get others. If we spend our time doing things that don't really count, we give up the time we could be using to perform important tasks. If we spend money on items of no value, we waste resources that could benefit those in need.

That Christmas, Hannah's parents bought Nana a very fitting shirt with this saying emblazoned on the front: "Nana is my name and spoiling is my game."

*"I praise you, Father . . . because you have hidden these things from the wise . . . and revealed them to little children."*

MATTHEW 11:25

In *The Power of a Positive Mom,* author Karol Ladd wrote these words. "Consider my friend, Victor Caballero, Jr. . . . Victor was one of ten children, raised from his youth by both his mother and grandmother in a household character-ized by both strict disci-pline and unconditional love. He credits these two women with the strength and determination he learned as a young man and which continue to serve him well now.

"More than anything else," Ladd further writes, "Victor says his mother and grandmother taught him the 'wisdom of compas-sion' and how to truly care for others. He adds, 'My mother and grandmother endured much pain in their lives, yet they were incredible pillars of strength mixed with kindness.'"[16]

> A grandchild is fed with cookies, milk, and praise.

As a grandparent, how can you show your grandkids unconditional love, strength, and kindness? Could you write them a note and have one of their parents place it in their backpacks before they go to school? Perhaps you could volunteer to tutor them in a subject they don't like or understand. Could you teach them the "wisdom of compassion"?

Would they be willing to help you make cookies for shut-ins or serve meals to the homeless? Would they like to tag along with you to visit a few elderly patients at the local nursing home? God will give us many ideas about ways to feed our grandchildren's souls, as well as their tummies. All we have to do is ask.

*Pleasant words are as an honeycomb,*
*sweet to the soul, and health to the bones.*
PROVERBS 16:24 KJV

GLDB

> A godly grandparent
> understands what a
> child does not say.

A young child looked up at his grandfather with wonder-filled eyes. "No *old* person has ever talked to *me* before," he announced. Grandpa realized what an unsettling thought that was. He wisely capitalized on this revelation and decided he would play checkers, tic-tac-toe, or do anything else in order to grab an opportunity to talk to his grandson. He soon found that thought-provoking questions opened the communication lines very well.

"Do you like everyone in your class?" he asked. "Is there someone in your class that nobody likes? Does it matter to you? Does it matter to that person? Is there anything you could do to help that child?" These kinds of questions can help us get into our grand-children's minds and understand them better.

It is a wise decision to play and talk with grandchildren often. While they play, we can ask them spiritual questions that will let us know if they have an awareness of God in their lives. We can teach them the importance of prayer and also the importance of listening when God has something to say to them. Telling them about Jesus is the greatest conversation we could ever have.

It's surprising how frequently children want to talk about deep thoughts when we open the door for them.

What a fun mission a grandparent can have if they will only take it! What an opportunity to influence the lives of those who come after us!

*He took the children in his arms, put his hands on them and blessed them.*
MARK 10:16

Connie often remembered the hot summer days when the kitchen would be steamy because her family was canning. Canning was a family affair. The men raised and harvested the crops; the children peeled, chopped, and prepared the produce; and the women cooked and did the actual canning. There was much lively discussion about recipes, techniques, and timing.

At some point during the day, Grandma would sneak Connie under the table and give her a taste of whatever was being canned. (She especially liked Grandma's pickled peaches.) Grandma would warn her to keep it their special secret. In fact, it was such a secret that Connie didn't find out until a few years ago that Grandma did this for all of her cousins and siblings. That discovery didn't make them love Grandma any less. It made them all feel special.

**In Grandma and Grandpa's eyes, everyone is the favorite!**

Because of it, Connie always thought she was Grandma's favorite grandchild, and that knowledge had sustained her through many rough times. When she found out that everyone in her generation thought they were Grandma's favorite grandchild, it didn't diminish that special feeling. She didn't feel betrayed. She was awed by the love that Grandma gave to the whole family. Her grandmother became the model for the kind of person she wanted to be.

God is the same way. He loves each one of us as if we were the only person in the universe. We are individually and personally His own special children.

Now as Connie makes gingerbread men with her own grandchildren, she passes along to them the knowledge that each and every one of them is as special to her as they are to God, and she prays that they will someday pass it along to their own grandchildren— maybe even in the kitchen.

*In truth I perceive that God shows no partiality.*
Acts 10:34 NKJV

Grandchildren are likely
to live up to what you
believe of them.

The West Point football team was defending their goal and had a six-point lead on the one-yard line. Coach Cahill was understandably anxious, but a linebacker said, "Don't worry, coach, they will not score!" They won the game because of a ferocious defense. The linebacker had power and wanted to win.

Ty Cobb positioned himself near the fence to catch a hard-hit ball. The ball was clearly beyond the fence and would have meant a home run with the bases loaded. However, in a ferocious demonstration of power, he took a backward dive over the fence and caught the ball. He had courage. He had power and wanted to win.

The humble Puritans had a different kind of power. They had an incredible amount of innter strength, along with tons of determination. They had strength of character that few of us have today. Why would they give up their homes in exchange for no home? Why would they face a stormy sea in a fragile ship? To them, the freedom to worship God as they pleased was worth every sacrifice they made. And they were determined to win.

Great coaches, like distinguished grandparents, work hard at their craft. Great things won't happen, however, by just doing what comes naturally. As grandparents, we can ignite the fire within our grandchildren to give them the power to understand that with God's help they can be winners at anything that they are determined to do.

*Be their ideal; let them follow the way you teach and live; be a pattern for them in your love, your faith, and your clean thoughts.*
1 TIMOTHY 4:12 TLB

To dye or not to dye, that was the question. Nana stood in front of the mirror and gazed at the person she had become. What had happened to the stark black hair and the tight skin on her face? The age spots were there, but she didn't feel that old. Where did they come from?

About that time, Pa walked into the room. He walked slower than he had in days past. Fortunately, his hair was still attached, but it was much grayer than it had once been. Nana remembered the words that she had spoken during their early years together. "I want to grow old with you." Suddenly, it dawned on her that she hadn't wanted it to happen quite this quickly.

> Grandparenting is a partnership with God.

She and Pa heard a cry come from the crib where their grandbaby had been sleeping. They both raced to pick her up. The baby smiled as they ran into the room. The grand-parents argued over who would "rescue" her from that mean old bed. Pa won the race and held the baby near his heart.

It dawned on Nana why she had wanted to grow old with Pa. He had been a wonderful father to their children and was showing signs of being a fabulous grandpa as well. She gazed into the mirror once again. The gray in her hair no longer mattered. The wrinkles were very small, and the age spots could be easily covered up.

Her husband, children, and grandchild loved her in spite of her age. And that was what mattered the most.

*A wife of noble character who can find?*
PROVERBS 31:10

> ## Never correct or criticize your grandchildren's parents in front of them.

In "Parenting for Parents," a chapter in Eric Wiggin's wonderful book, *The Gift of Grandparenting,* the author says grandparents must learn to "separate sensitive, personal advice from impersonal advice. Realize that what you may consider impersonal may be taken personally by someone with differing thought processes. To point out that your son-in-law's car, which is belching black smoke, probably needs the choke cleaned may be taken as suggesting he's a polluter and somewhat of a slob.

"Or he may be grateful to know that a stuck choke might be fixed with a $1.59 can of solvent and an old toothbrush, since a mechanic has just quoted $300 for a carburetor overhaul, which his car probably does not need."

So what's appropriate to do when a worry arises? Pray about your concerns first. If you still feel that you need to mention something, try to do it when the grandchildren aren't around. Don't be demanding or approach your adult child with a "my way is the only way" attitude. Lovingly, address the issue and then let it go.

Wiggin also suggests asking yourself, "Is my grandchild going to be seriously harmed by my withholding advice?" or "Do I have constructive criticism, or am I just airing worries?" He says grandparents should give their adult children time and space to grow into their parenting responsibilities. It is also important to remember that God is ultimately in control of all things.[17]

*Do not speak evil of one another, brethren.*
JAMES 4:11 NKJV

A grandmother asked her granddaughter if she would like to go to the pet store to see the puppies. The four-year-old child responded with absolute glee.

"All right, then," the grandmother replied. "If you are good tonight when we go out, I will take you to see puppies tomorrow after school. We'll have a wonderful time!"

The child agreed and later, when Grandmother said it was time to get their shoes on so they could go out for the night, the child ran to her bedroom. She returned with her shoes proudly placed on the wrong feet.

"I'm ready!" she exclaimed. "I'm ready to go see puppies!"

**Always keep your promises!**

Somehow the child had missed the point, but Grandmother had not. The child focused on the promise rather than the payment. However, promises go two ways. The child promised to be good, and Grandmother had promised to take her to see the puppies.

That evening, the child exemplified perfect behavior. The next day, Grandmother took her to the pet store. The delight on the child's face became the icing on the cake. But better than that was the knowledge that her granddaughter would always trust her grandmother's word in all seasons and in every circumstance, both large and small. A little gift of a promise reaps big rewards and earns a great deal of trust.

*Like clouds and wind without rain*
*is a man who boasts of gifts he does not give.*
PROVERBS 25:14

## There's no place like home—except Grandma's.

One Sunday afternoon, a grandmother went to run a few errands. She noticed as she got into the car that dozens of birds were in a tree in her backyard. During that particular time of the year, the tree had hundreds of berries on each limb. She was surprised that the limbs hadn't broken since they were so heavy.

Birds of every species and color flew from one limb to another. It seemed they were having a big family reunion, while eating the berries. They were also singing joyful songs, as they feasted on the delicious fruit.

She realized that just like that tree was a gathering place for the birds, her home was a gathering place for her family. When her children and grandchildren came to visit, she provided them with extra special treats and meals fit for kings and queens. A few weekends earlier, she had entertained most of her children. They laughed and shared things that were important to them.

Then it dawned on her that her children hadn't come for the food they would eat, although they enjoyed it when they arrived. They came just to spend some time together, as a family. They came to laugh, to look at old pictures, and to reminisce about times gone by.

While the berries on the tree had attracted the birds, the love in the home was what had attracted the children and grandchildren. Since they live several hours apart, she knows that she won't get everybody all together often, but when she does, their presence will put a song in her heart that will last for weeks at a time.

Make love the main attraction in your home!

*Surely goodness and love will follow me*
*all the days of my life.*
PSALM 23:6

In an episode of *The Andy Griffith Show,* young Opie finds a wallet that contains fifty dollars. It holds no identification. He takes the wallet to his father, Sheriff Taylor, who places an advertisement in the paper.

"If no one claims the wallet in a week," Sheriff Taylor says, "the money belongs to you." The week slowly passes by, and at the end of the week, nobody has claimed the wallet. Opie becomes fifty dollars richer.

> Being honest is the best-paying character trait we can portray.

Wisely, Andy encourages his son to spend ten dollars on himself and put the remaining forty dollars in his piggy bank. Opie agrees and goes to purchase a fishing pole. He returns to the courthouse to show his father his new fishing gear. But his father is not there. Parnell Rigby, the owner of the wallet, is in the courthouse waiting for Sheriff

Taylor to return. Parnell tells Opie about how he has lost his wallet. Opie has a decision to make. He could remain quiet and keep his fishing pole or take the pole back and return all the money to Mr. Rigby.

When Opie's father arrives home, he sees a broken piggy bank. A little while later, he sees his son leaving the hardware store. He assumes that Opie has gone against his instructions and spent the remainder of the money. Imagine his surprise when he learns about Opie's honest decision.

"Opie," Andy says, "you're something else. Did you know that? You're something else."[18]

When we see that our children or grandchildren have performed a commendable act, we should be ready to let them know how proud we are of them. Our encouragement will motivate them to continue developing godly character.

*A good man is known by his truthfulness;*
*a false man by deceit and lies.*
PROVERBS 12:17 TLB

> Never make a promise
> before you check with your
> grandchild's parents.

Nan and her sisters enjoyed living on a farm, although they grew up poor. Every day during the summer and fall, they played barefoot in the creek near their house and daydreamed while watching the clouds drift through the sky. It helped them take their minds off the problems in their home. Their father was an alcoholic, and their mom worked numerous hours each week.

When Nan's grandmother "Gram," who lived on a cotton farm nearby, asked the girls to help her pick the rest of the cotton crop, they jumped at the chance to do something different. She promised to pay them for each day they worked. They were thrilled to have the opportunity to earn a little spending money.

The girls worked hard. By the time they were finished each evening, their hands were raw. Their backs and feet ached from the standing and bending. But each day when they went to pick up their money from Gram, she made excuses for not paying them.

"Your father owes me money," she said many times. "I'll pay you when he pays me." Their grandmother never paid them for their hard work.

Now Nan is a fifty-five-year-old grandmother of three.

"I still have trouble trusting people," she says. "I can't trust even the people that I dearly love. My parents hurt me, and my grandmother took advantage of me. But I learned from my grandmother's bad example that keeping a promise to my grandchildren is extremely important."

Be sure and keep the promises you make to your grandchildren!

*Now it is required that those who have been given a trust must prove faithful.*
1 CORINTHIANS 4:2

Four-year-old Becky loved going to Papa's house. One day Papa took her fishing. Her big brothers loved to fish too, so he let them go along as well. Becky's daddy, Roy, didn't like fishing, but since everybody else was going, he agreed to go too.

While Papa dug for bait and got the fishing poles ready, Roy folded up the high chair and put it in the truck. He didn't want Becky standing in the tall grass.

Finally, everybody was ready to go. They headed toward the fishing hole. Everyone threw out a line and fought mosquitoes. They watched the corks for what seemed like hours to Roy. He grumbled while he sat there beside Becky. Finally, Becky got a bite and pulled the line. A tiny fish was on the end of it. She squealed in delight.

**Always let your grandchildren know you love them just the way they are.**

Her daddy took the fish off the hook and threw it on the ground. It flopped up and down. Becky started to cry. "Throw it back," she cried. "Throw it back." Since it was too small to eat, Roy threw the fish back into the water. He baited her hook again, and as luck would have it, she caught another fish. The scenario was the same, however, and Roy threw the second fish back—and each subsequent catch. Totally aggravated, the men packed it up and returned to the house empty-handed.

Sometimes when grandkids are around, things don't always turn out like expected, but pleasant memories can be formed with each visit. Twenty-two years later, the family continues to laugh about what Becky considered the perfect fishing trip—"catch 'em and throw 'em back."

Enjoy your grandchildren—just as they are.

*You made him ruler over the works of your hands . . . the birds of the air, and the fish of the sea.*
PSALM 8:6,8

## A spoiled grandchild may too soon become a little stinker.

Kathleen's parents raised her in a loving and strict home. While she never lacked for anything, she was given chores to complete and was forced to take on certain responsibilities in the home. Her parents demanded respect. Kathleen sang in the choir. She was popular among her fellow students and faculty. After her graduation, she left home to study law.

Years later, Kathleen met the man of her dreams. She was married, and years later she became a mother. When their son Timothy was born, Kathleen's parents adored him.

Kathleen left her law practice to become a full-time mother. Timothy demanded her constant attention with his rambunctious way. She didn't mind the challenge, however, as she loved being a stay-at-home mother. She employed the same parenting methods that her parents had used while raising her.

Kathleen and two-year-old Timothy spent an afternoon with her parents. Timmy became disobedient to his mother. Kathleen patiently asked him to behave. After another disrespectful encounter, Kathleen took him to the back room for discipline. Moments later, mother and child returned to find Grandmother in tears.

"It breaks my heart when you have to discipline him," Kathleen's mother sobbed.

"Mom, I am trying to raise Timmy like you and Dad raised me. It's the highest compliment I can give to you," Kathleen said.

"I can do nothing but respect that," Kathleen's mother said. "You are right."

Be thankful when your grandchildren receive discipline that helps them to learn.

*A fool spurns his father's discipline,*
*but whoever heeds correction shows prudence.*
PROVERBS 15:5

In *The Grandmother Book,* Betty Southard and Jan Stoop wrote, "It's not easy to be a listening grandmother, but oh, it is so rewarding!" They listed several traits that good- listener grandparents share:

A good listener tries to hear the feelings behind the words that are spoken. Many times, body language and tone say much more than words. Are you listening with your eyes, as well as your ears?

A good listener echoes back what she hears. According to the authors, this is called active listening. "Not only does it require you to check out the accuracy of what you have heard, it also requires you to concentrate more on what the

> **Always take time to listen to and encourage your grandchildren.**

child is saying than on how you are going to respond."

A good listener resists the temptation to jump in with a quick fix. Do you tend to want to "fix" your grandchildren's problems? Try counting to ten after each statement they make, and then ask, "What do you need from me right now?" or "How can I help?" They may only want you to listen at that time.

A good listener knows her limits. Healthy adults set healthy boundaries. If you become overwhelmed, say so.

A good listener has to work at it. Listening is rarely a God-given gift. Instead, it is cultivated by time and practice.[19]

Listen to your grandchildren. They will love you for it.

*Encourage one another and build each other up, just as in fact you are doing.*
1 THESSALONIANS 5:11

> Let all your words, either
> written or spoken,
> come from your heart.

There's nothing any more endearing or innocent than the words that come from the heart of a child. The following letter written by a granddaughter to her grandparents are words to be treasured:

Dear Grandma and Grandpa,

Do you know what I like best about coming to your house? I like what I learn when I'm watching you two. Every morning, Grandma, you read your Bible. I see this, and I wonder if that may be why you can make good cookies. Grandpa, I think that when you go on your morning walks, you're chatting with God. Is that why you are wise? And before meals we say the blessing at your house. I like that.

Sometimes around here we don't get to eat a meal as a family, much less say the blessing.

I have never heard bad words come out of your mouths either. Even when Grandma's biscuits burned or when Grandpa hit his thumb with the hammer, neither of you said bad things. You get upset, but you don't allow things like that to change the way you talk.

I also like going to church with you on Sundays and Wednesdays. The potluck dinners are cool. Grandma, when you overheard Mrs. Simmons talking about your casserole, you didn't try to get even. I notice things like that.

Grandpa once said that a life well lived may be the only Gospel some people ever hear. Well, if that's true, you are both living Gospels.

> I love you,
> Your granddaughter

*You are our epistle written in our hearts,*
*known and read by all men.*
2 CORINTHIANS 3:2 NKJV

In 1991, George Gallup completed a poll entitled, "The Saints among Us." According to the results, only 10 percnt of American Christians were considered "deeply committed." An even smaller percentage of people earned the right to be referred to as having "high spiritual faith." Gallup referred to these few people as a breed apart. "They are more tolerant of people with diverse backgrounds. They are absolutely committed to prayer. They are far, far happier than the rest of the population," noted Mr. Gallup.[20]

**Prayer changes things.**

Many times we read phrases such as "a need to be committed to prayer" as though it were some difficult task hanging over our heads or a necessary, but cumbersome, part of the Christian life. Forced prayer can sometimes feel that way. The natural process of prayer is much easier. Speaking to God while walking step by step with Him is the greatest way to pray.

If we ask any grandparents if they would rather give their grandchild the recent hot-ticket item at the toy store or would rather be dedicated to pray for that child for the rest of their lives, Mr. Gallup may find that the statistics will go up. And if the grandparents would actually take the time to pray for their grandchildren on a daily basis, future generations would be greatly blessed.

What greater gift could any grandparent give to their grandchildren than to pray for them daily?

Barbie dolls and Tonka trucks come and go. Prayer lasts a lifetime.

*Devote yourselves to prayer, keeping alert in it with an attitude of thanksgiving.*
COLOSSIANS 4:2 NASB

God, grant me the senility to forget the people I dislike, the good fortune to encounter those I like, and the eyesight to be able to tell the difference.

Amanda and John decided they needed more friends.

"I want someone to come to my funeral!" Amanda laughingly told John.

John considered Amanda's statement, agreed with her, and invited several couples over for dinner. He cooked one of his delicious gourmet meals. The couple made a habit of staying in touch with their friends and inviting them over on a regular basis.

"The only problem now is that John invites so many people to our house that I sometimes have company when I'm not there!" says Amanda, with a shake of her head.

In the same way, when we can, we should consider our time with our grandchildren as a valuable treasure. We should look for opportunities to play with them and become a big part of their young lives. While at the playground, we can even find other people our own age playing with their grandchildren. Anyone who has a grandchild has a common interest right off the bat.

Karen Burton Mains wrote these words in *Friends and Strangers:* "I am well aware now that the greatest secret about strangers is that any one of them may become a friend, one who will not forget me, nor abandon me when I am troubled, nor lie to me when I need the truth."[21]

*The LORD bless you and keep you;*
*the LORD make his face shine upon you*
*and be gracious to you;*
*the LORD turn his face toward you*
*and give you peace.*
NUMBERS 6:24-26

When movie stars are invited to place their hands and feet in wet cement outside Mann's Chinese Theatre on Hollywood Boulevard, it is a tremendous honor and an occasion worthy of celebration. They know they are permanently leaving their mark in that place.

They are very careful while leaving their imprints. There are guards present to stand by to protect the prints until they have dried. The stars never carelessly plop their hands and feet down indifferently. They want to leave beautiful imprints that will last forever.

> Grandchildren are like wet cement— whatever falls on them makes an impression.

Grandparents should approach their grandchildren with the same tender loving care and consideration. Grandparents are capable of leaving marks on a grandchild's character that will last a lifetime. What a tremendous responsibility and privilege!

Good grandparents are cognizant of the imprints they are making in the lives of their grandchildren and are aware of their feelings, perceptions, and sensitivities. In many ways, grandparents represent the love of Christ to their grandchildren.

Through the life of grandparents, grandchildren can learn about God's character and about His great love for the world. They can learn the true meaning of the word *Christian*. By example, grandparents should let their grandchildren see them as they live godly lives full of integrity, compassion, and love. It is a tremendous honor and an occasion worthy of celebration when people become grandparents. They are leaving their mark on a child's heart that will last forever.

What kind of mark are you leaving on your grandchildren's lives?

*Follow my example, as I follow*
*the example of Christ.*
1 CORINTHIANS 11:1

GLDB

> Grandchildren do as we do,
> so we should be careful
> what we do.

Grandma was playing with her eighteen-month-old granddaughter in the living room late one afternoon. They were singing "I'm a Little Teapot." When Grandma stood straight up, so did her granddaughter. The little girl copied her grandmother when she leaned over sideways to "pour the tea out," while singing the song.

About that time, Grandpa walked into the room, picked up a tissue, and blew his nose. His granddaughter stopped what she was doing. She pulled another tissue from the box, covered her face, and blew her nose too.

Children are imitators of adults. They see and hear everything. To a child, whatever the adult does is perfectly fine. A grandparent should be aware that little eyes are watching them and little ears hear everything that is said—good or bad. The way we lead our lives should be worthy of imitation.

When Jesus came to the world in the form of a man, He was the perfect example of how we should live our lives. In Ephesians 5:1 we read these words: "Be imitators of God, therefore, as dearly loved children."

Jesus showed a great deal of love and compassion while He walked here on Earth. He was kind and considerate. He sacrificed greatly, even to the point of death. What do our actions tell our grandchildren? How would we feel if we caught them imitating the things that we do or repeating the words we use?

*Be kind and compassionate*
*to one another.*
EPHESIANS 4:32

Don Hall, head of Hallmark, Inc., was introduced before speaking to a group of his employees. The master of ceremonies gave a lengthy introduction of this very impressive man. She spoke of Mr. Hall's many business achievements and community activities. Near the end of the lengthy introduction, the emcee noted briefly the number of Hall's children and grandchildren.

As the applause faded, Hall stepped to the microphone to address his audience. "I apologize for that introduction," Hall laughed. "It seems to get longer every time I stand before a group of people. The only important thing in that entire speech, however, is the number of grandchildren I have."

> **Memories, not money, make us rich.**

After Hall's speech concluded, the audience was highly impressed. It was not the successful company that he had helped to build that impressed them. It wasn't the fact that the company had showed a profit every year since Don's father founded it in 1910. Instead, his employees were awed by the love he showed for his grandchildren and his clear sense of priorities.

Grandparenthood is a time when people tend to take stock of their lives, to evaluate whether they have been successful. We may never be able to match Don Hall's accomplishments as businesspeople. Nevertheless, if we love our grandchildren and understand that they are more important than status, power, or material wealth, we will be every bit as successful as Don is—and just as wise too.

*Children's children are a crown to the aged.*
PROVERBS 17:6

> The most precious of
> all days is the day your
> child's child is born.

Pa and Nana drove almost three hours one Sunday afternoon to their son's house. As they drove, they chattered constantly about what the next day would bring. "Do you realize that this time tomorrow we're going to be grandparents?" Nana asked.

"Does that mean we're getting old?" Pa replied.

"Nope, it just means we're getting better. We're going to have another little person in our lives to love us as we get older. She will bring joy to our lives and hope to our future."

The next day, the entire family went to the hospital for the scheduled cesarean section. The family paced around the waiting room while Chad and Lucy went to the operating room. At the sound of a squeaking bassinet rolling down the hallway, everybody ran to greet the newest member of the family.

"This is Hannah Marie," Chad announced as he put his arm around his mom. "She has your middle name!"

"Hannah, this is Nana," she said through tears of joy. Hannah screamed at the top of her lungs.

That was one of the greatest days that Nana and Pa ever shared together. Being a grand-parent is an awesome blessing and a special gift given by God. There are no words that can describe the initial feeling that grandparents feel when, for the first time, they look into the eyes of their grandchildren.

It can be an instant feeling of love, devotion, and gratitude all tied together in one pink, or sometimes one blue, bow.

Do you remember the first time you met each grandchild? Spend a moment thanking God for those special times.

*Give thanks to the LORD, for he is good;*
*his love endures forever.*
PSALM 118:1

Helen Keller was once asked how she would approach old age. She responded:

Age seems to be only another physical handicap, and it excites no dread in me. Once I had a dear friend of eighty, who impressed upon me the fact that he enjoyed life more than he had done at twenty-five. "Never count how many years you have, as the French say," he would insist, "but how many interests you have. Do not stale your days by taking for granted the people about you, or the things which make up your environment, and you will ever abide in a realm of fadeless beauty."

> It's not how old you are, but how you are old.

The poem "How Old Are You?" reinforces this idea that *outlook* determines our age:

Age is a quality of mind:
If you have left your dream behind,
If hope is cold
If you no longer look ahead,
If your ambition fires are dead—
Then you are old.
But if from life you take the best,
And if in life you keep the jest,
If love you hold;
No matter how the years go by,
No matter how the birthdays fly,
You are not old.[22]

Years before we reach what we would call "old age," we determine whether that time will be a gracious and pleasant time or a time of bitterness.

No time is too late to practice the attitudes of youth. Start today. Count your blessings, do something fun, and call your grandchildren to see how they are doing.

*The righteous flourish like the palm tree. . . .*
*They still bring forth fruit in old age.*
PSALM 92:12,14 RSV

# Grandparents know
# how to live young!

Sometimes it seems that life is lived backwards! When we are young and have only limited perspective, we have to make the huge decisions of life that will shape the rest of our years. But we can—and are wise to—learn from those who have gained insight from life's experiences.

In a sociological study, fifty people over the age of ninety-five were asked the question: "If you could live your life over again, what would you do differently?" Three general responses emerged from the questionnaire,

"If I had it to do over again . . .

I would reflect more.

I would risk more.

I would do more things that would live on after I am dead."

An elderly woman wrote this about how she would live her life if she had it to live over again:

"I'd make more mistakes next time; I'd relax; I would limber up; I would be sillier than I have been this trip; I would take fewer things seriously; I would take more chances; I would climb more mountains and swim more rivers; I would eat more ice cream and less beans; I would perhaps have more actual troubles, but I'd have fewer imaginary ones.

"You see, I'm one of those people who lives sensibly and sanely hour after hour, day after day. Oh, I've had my moments, and if I had it to do over again, I'd have more of them. In fact, I'd try to do nothing else, just moments, one after the other instead of living so many years ahead of time."

Listen and learn! Life cannot be all work and no play, yet you want your life to be meaningful to God, to your loved ones who follow you, and to yourself.

Reflect on your life. Ask God to show you the true meaning of your existence, what you are to accomplish—and how to have fun along the way!

*Incline your ear to wisdom,*
*And apply your heart to understanding.*
PROVERBS 2:2 NKJV

# Acknowledgments

1. *Shadowlands.* Director: Richard Attenborough, Screen play: William Nicholson, Producers Richard Attenborough and Brian Eastman. Savoy Pictures, 1993.

2. Lewis, C.S., *A Grief Observed,* (New York: Bantam Books, 1961).

3. Lee Pitts, "These Things I Wish for Each of You," *People Who Live at the End of Dirt Roads* (Morro Bay, CA: Lee Pitts, 1995).

4. Nancy Gibbs, *Prayerfully Yours, from a Mom's Heart to You!* (Kearney, Nebraska: Morris Publishing, 2002), p. 64.

5. "Personal Glimpses," "Come on Down," *Reader's Digest,* October 2001, p. 59.

6. Anne Morrow Lindbergh, "Introduction," *Hour of Gold, Hour of Lead* (New York, NY Harcourt Brace, 1973).

7. Cindy Morgan, *Barefoot on Barbed Wire: A Journey out of Fear into Freedom* (Eugene, Oregon: Harvest House Publishers, 2001).

8. Janet Colsher Teitsort, *Long Distance Gramma* (Grand Rapids: Baker Book House, 1998).

9. Clem Boyd, Web page: "The Vacation Connection," Web site: Focus Over Fifty: A Web site of Focus on the Family. Web address: *www.family.org/focusoverfifty/justforyou/a0012678.html.*

10. Betty Southard and Jan Stoop, *The Grandmother Book* (Nashville: Thomas Nelson, 1993).

[11] Elisa Morgan, editor, *NIV Mom's Devotional Bible* (Grand Rapids: Zondervan, 1997).

[12] Carole Mayhall, *Words that Hurt, Words that Heal* (Colorado Springs: NavPress, 1986).

[13] Karen O'Connor, *Basket of Blessings: 31 Days to a More Grateful Heart* (Waterbrook Press, 1998).

[14] Eva Marie Everson, *One True Vow: Love Stories of Faith and Commitment* (Promise Press, 2001).

[15] Florence Littauer, et al, *A Letter Is a Gift Forever: The Charm and Tradition of a Handwritten Note* (Harvest House, 2001).

[16] Karol Ladd, *The Power of a Positive Mom* (West Monroe, Louisiana: Howard Publishing Company, 2001).

[17] Eric Wiggin, Gary D. Chapman, *The Gift of Grandparenting: Building Meaningful Relationships with Your Grandchildren* (Carol Stream, Illinois: Tyndale House Publishers, 2001).

[18] Episode 136: "Opie's Fortune" (B/W), *The Andy Griffith Show,* written by Ben Joelson and Art Baer. Directed by Coby Ruskin (1964-65 season).

[19] Betty Southard and Jan Stoop, *The Grandmother Book.*

[20] Author unknown, title unknown, *The Houston Post* (July 6, 1991, p. E-3).

[21] Karen Burton Mains, *Friends and Strangers: Divine Encounters in Lonely Places* (Dallas: Word, 1990).

[22] Walter B. Knight, *Knight's Master Book of 4,000 Illustrations* (Grand Rapids, MI: Eerdmans Publishing Co., 1956), p. 448 and ibid.

Additional copies of this book and other titles in the
*God's Little Devotional Book* series are
available from your local bookstore.
Also look for our special gift editions in this series.

*God's Little Devotional Book for Dads*
*God's Little Devotional Book for Graduates*
*God's Little Devotional Book for Men*
*God's Little Devotional Book for Moms*
*God's Little Devotional Book for Students*
*God's Little Devotional Book for Teachers*
*God's Little Devotional Book for Teens*
*God's Little Devotional Book for Women*

If you have enjoyed this book,
or if it has impacted your life,
we would like to hear from you.
Please contact us at:
Honor Books
An Imprint of Cook Communications Ministries
4050 Lee Vance View
Colorado Springs, CO 80918

Or by email at cookministries.com